TRAP HISTORY

ATLANTA CULTURE AND THE GLOBAL IMPACT OF TRAP MUSIC

A.R. SHAW

Trap History: Atlanta Culture and the Global Impact of Trap Music. by A.R. Shaw

Copyright© 2020 by A.R. Shaw. All rights reserved, including the right to reproduce this book or portions thereof in any form whatsoever. For information, contact:
Bluefield Media, LLC.
P.O. Box 310626
2260 Fairburn Rd, Atlanta Georgia 30331.
First Edition November 2020.

Our books may be purchased in bulk for promotional, educational, or business use. A.R. Shaw can also be booked for speaking engagements. Please Contact Email (arshawmedia@aol.com).

Visit www.traphistory.com

First Edition November 2020.

Cover Artwork: Soweto Bosia, Kareem Kenyada, Joe Moss. Cover Photo: Louis Cuthbert. Book Layout: Robert Lee. Cover Subject: Mare of NEA Records and Brittney Keith.

Layout: Robert D. Lee

Interior Photos by: A.R. Shaw.

The Library of Congress Cataloging-in-Publication Data is available upon request.

ISBN (paperback) 978-0-9789799-6-6
ISBN (ebook) 0-9789799-6-6

FROM THE AUTHOR

Dear Reader,

This book is intended to share the story of an American city that captivated the world through its culture, music, style, art and hard work. Thank you for taking this journey with me. I hope these stories inspire the next generation of cultural innovators and future leaders who can inspire change. -A.R. Shaw

INTRODUCTION
PART I: THE MUSIC
Chapter I
Welcome to Traplanta
Chapter II
How Strip Club Culture & Bass Music Gave Rise to Southern Rap
Chapter III
OutKast, the era of Crunk, and Atlanta's Epic Nightlife
Chapter IV
From Snap to Trap: The Life and Times of Shawty Lo
Chapter V
Trap Becomes Music: The Journey of T.I.
Chapter VI
The Rise of Trap Music: Jeezy, the BMF Takeover, and the era of Mixtapes
Chapter VII
Gucci Mane: The Plug to Trap Music Stardom
Chapter VIII
How Migos' *Culture* Album Changed the Culture of Trap Music

PART II: THE TRAP
Chapter IX
Welcome to the Bluff -
The World's Most Notorious Trap
Chapter X
Trapped in Addiction:
Mental Health and Trap Music
Chapter XI
Trapped by Circumstance:
Rap's Death Trap
Chapter XII
Gentrifying the Trap

PART III: BEYOND THE TRAP
Chapter XIII
Trap Monuments
Chapter XIV
Trappin' Around the World
Chapter XV
Trap - American Music.
American Problem. American Dream.

I

INTRODUCTION

A.R. Shaw

Art by Kareem Kenyada.
Concept by A.R. Shaw.

Shackles and chains have always served as symbols of oppression in the place known as the land of the free. From slave ships that arrived in 1619 to the men and women currently imprisoned, the capturing of black bodies and the bondage of black souls represent how fundamental rights and freedom can be a fleeting reality. Following the abolition of slavery, black communities remained under siege. The bombing of Black Wall Street in Tulsa, Oklahoma in 1921; the thousands of black people who were lynched in the South; the influx of crack cocaine and guns into black communities in the 1980s; and the millions of black citizens who became the property of the state or government as mass incarceration took hold of a nation. Indeed, black bodies in captivity is engrained in the fabric of the United States of America.

Before one word was ever written for this book, a vision came to me in the form of two hands. One hand would symbolize the freedom that most young black people hope to obtain through the means of music, art, and creativity. The right hand clutched a microphone as it represented the ability to be heard while living amongst the voiceless. That same hand would be adorned with a diamond-encrusted ring on its pinky finger and a diamond-encrusted watch around the wrist. On the left hand, a dime-bag of drugs is held tightly by the index finger and thumb. Similar to the microphone, the drugs can also be viewed as a source of power, manipulation, and access to income. A single handcuff is locked around the left wrist. The handcuff and diamond-encrusted watch are both chained together creating restrictions and a sense of togetherness for both hands. At some point, each hand uses the other as a means to survive. Both hands represent the subjugation of a group of people seeking any form of escapism, whether it be through music or the distribution or use of narcotics. The hands represent the essence of what it means to be trapped by desires and circumstances.

We were the kids of Atlanta. Born and raised in a city that seemed like an island located in the South, but not of the South. Our dialect and manners were traditionally Southern, but we did not give a damn about certain Southern traditions that suggested minorities accept second-class status. Atlanta served as our oasis, a destination where the young and inspired could find refuge. We could dream like Martin, inspire change like Maynard, and create like the Dungeon Family. We were from the bottom but always believed that we had a puncher's chance to reach the top. It only took one song, one acceptance letter, one scholarship, one employment opportunity, or one business idea for our lives to change forever. To walk in Atlanta often meant that you were walking on the power of possibility.

From a music standpoint, history worked in our favor. The first black-owned radio station in America (WERD) opened its doors on Atlanta's historic Auburn

Avenue in 1949. And the first person to reference the words "rock and roll" on a song was a black woman born in Atlanta named Trixie Smith. Smith used the phrase in 1922 on the song "My Daddy Rocks Me." The term "rock and roll" would eventually morph into the popular music genre inspired largely by blues musicians from the South. Other Georgians like Ray Charles, Gladys Knight, and James Brown would forever change the face of R&B and soul. In the words of culture curator Bem Joiner, "Atlanta influences everything."

But even hope in its highest form would not allow Atlanta to escape the failures of the South entirely. Regardless of the steps we marched, the distances we ran, and the heights we reached, the unforgiving faults of the South hovered over Atlanta like a dark cloud before an April thunderstorm. Our pride and culture could not prevent us from becoming victims of its inescapable wrath. We were a city of progression in the least progressive region in America.

The South can feel like a place where tradition reigns and justice for all arrives at a snail's pace, that's if the truth ever gets a chance to reach its destination. Cotton fields and large farms that continue to operate under the name "plantation" provide evidence of a time where black labor was free. The notion that railroad tracks can serve as barriers in the segregation of small towns remains a reality for some areas in Georgia still beholden to the ideas of Jim Crow where you would only need to travel a few miles outside of the metro Atlanta area to experience this reality up close. This is the new and old normal of living life in the Dirty

South, a place that gave birth to Trap music.

Trap music stands as one of the most popular genres to emerge in rap. But Trap music is more than 808 beats and lyrics; it is music that derives from a location. The Trap is a term coined in Atlanta as a place where drugs are sold, bought, and used. Trap music is a form of rap that reveals how the war on drugs affects poor and disenfranchised communities. The story of Trap music begins with the story of Atlanta.

By the 1980s, Atlanta benefited from a rich history as the birthplace of Dr. Martin Luther King, Jr. and a key location for the Civil Rights Movement. A world-class airport made it one of the most important cities in America as Mayor Maynard Jackson's initiative to include black-owned businesses in all city contracts created a substantial black upper-middle class. By 1990, the International Olympic Committee found Atlanta to be the perfect destination for the 1996 Olympics. But the newsworthy achievements were only a glorified bandage that could never heal Atlanta's permanent scars.

The Atlanta Child Murders gave us chills even after the arrest of Wayne Williams—the 23-year-old man who was convicted of killing two adult males in 1982. But the murders of more than 20 black kids from 1979-1981 remained unsolved, leaving most of the victims' families and a city without a satisfying resolution.

We were also reminded of the ghosts of Jim Crow with a state flag that hung above us when we entered our schools, public facilities, and even some religious institutions. The Confederate flag flew as Georgia's official state flag from 1956 until 2001. Even when our homegrown heroes such as A.T. Walden, John Wesley Dobbs, W.E.B. Du Bois, John Lewis, Xernona Clayton Brady, Dr. Alonzo Crim, Joseph Lowery, C.T. Vivian, Hosea Williams, Coretta Scott King, and Dr. Martin Luther King, Jr. taught us how and when to fight, most of us remained at a disadvantage. Decades after the height of the Civil Rights Movement, Atlanta continued to be one of the most segregated cities in America, separated by race and economic opportunities.

Housing segregation became a reality sponsored by the United States government as banks and mortgage lenders systemically prevented the flow of wealth from entering black communities. The 1938 Home Owner's Loan Corporation "Residential Security Map" of Atlanta revealed how lenders made it a point to practice racial discrimination. Appraisers awarded a grade of A or B to white neighborhoods with high levels of racial restrictions on the sale of the property. And it gave grades of C or D to areas where most Blacks resided. The redlining ensured that most blacks could only obtain housing in those designated communities. In turn, the distribution of wealth in Atlanta was severely skewed in the decades following 1938.

Today, Atlanta leads the nation in income inequality. In 2020, the median household income for white families in Atlanta was $83,722, compared to a $28,105 median income for black families. If a child in Atlanta is raised in poverty, there is only a four percent chance that he or she will escape poverty by the age of thirty.

The outcome of such damage reshaped Atlanta and gave rise to the Trap and, eventually, Trap music. Although its origins are Southern-based, the music and sound influenced artists across America and around the world.

I recall first hearing the word "Trap" as a slang term during the early 1990s. Before it evolved into music, Trap was a place, an action, and a mentality that grew from Atlanta's inner-city communities.

From a geographical standpoint, certain areas in Atlanta are so secluded that they are structured similarly to a Trap. Due to a history of bad urban planning, a multitude of one-way streets, dead-end roads, and cul-de-sacs exist in Atlanta. When white settlers in Georgia forced the Creek and Cherokee Indians from their land in the 1820s, the Georgia land lottery system allowed white settlers to purchase plots of land for as little as 25 cents. But as the city, then known as Terminus, began to expand and become the railroad capital of the South, landowners increased their profits by only allocating a minimum amount of land for streets. As a result, the city of Atlanta was never built on a logical grid system. If you were to look at a map of Atlanta, you would notice that many of the streets resemble tangled wires or a plate of spaghetti. Many of the roads in Atlanta begin and end without any rhyme or reason.

The dozens of dead-end streets and cul-de-sacs in the city became key locations for drug dealers who used the isolated areas as the Trap. Those who dared to venture inside of a drug Trap understood the possible captivity of entering because there was usually only one way in and one way out. The Trap was a place strictly reserved for the buyers and sellers of drugs. In turn, the act of dealing in the Trap became known as "Trapping." The Trap also became indicative of a mentality. Trauma can occur when groups of people live in desperate environments with subpar education, a lack of job opportunities, and resources to succeed. Those who sold and bought drugs were often trapped by the idea of the Trap as the only place that life could offer them.

While growing up in southwest, Atlanta, I viewed the term "Trap" as just another example of how we expressed ourselves in the city. We had our own dances, our own style of dress, and our own ways to communicate. So when we discussed the "Trap" or "Trapping," we were only playing by the rules of our own environment. At the time, I never really thought about how our slang and culture would impact the world until I got a chance to see the world.

In the summer of 2012, I took my first trip to Europe to cover the Olympics in London for the black-owned Atlanta-based publication, *Rolling Out* magazine. After covering several events, a colleague and I decided to visit a bar and restaurant located near London Stadium. At some point during the evening, we started a conversation with two women in their mid-20s. They suggested we go to a nightclub near Brixton where the DJ mostly played hip-hop and Afrobeat music. But on some evenings, the women told us, the club's promoters would feature a party known as "Trap Night."

The women continued to name other nightclubs that we should visit, but my mind drifted away from the conversation as I attempted to make sense of Trap music in London. Black American music has always found its way into Europe. From the jazz scene that took over in the 1920s to New York hip-hop's influence in the 1980s, black music remains one of America's greatest exports. But Trap music seemed different due to its underground element. Hip-hop proved to be global, but Trap music was a sound and style of rap specific to Atlanta at the time. The Brits likely got their first dose of Trap music in the mid-2000s when artists such as T.I. and Young Jeezy gained mainstream success. But I wondered if those who embraced Trap music understood its origins.

Trap music provides a glimpse of the Trap, but some listeners may not understand how it relates to everyday life. Some may not identify with the people who were raised on Simpson Road in Atlanta and viewed Trapping as the only way to pay bills. They may not relate to the mothers who lived in Bankhead Courts who worried as their kids walked past drug dealers and drug users while in route to their school bus. And they may not be able to understand the plight of a person who lived only to get high in a Trap on the Westside of Atlanta known as the Bluff. There are drug dealers who worked days and nights on street corners just to earn a salary close to or less than minimum wage. There are real-life consequences for the drug addicts who are ripped from families and only live to cop the next high. And some hard-working residents witnessed the decline of their neighborhood once it became a drug Trap.

Atlanta natives found ways to transform hopelessness into art. The city inspired the poetics of OutKast; the dope boy thoughts of T.I.; the Trap star dreams of Jeezy; the Trap mentality of Gucci Mane; the melodic pain of Future; and the anomalous flow of Migos.

Before Trap music became branded as a genre, the

drug trade in black communities was highlighted in early rap songs such as N.W.A's "Dope Man"; KRS-One's "Love's Gonna Get You"; Public Enemy's "Night of the Living Baseheads"; UGK's "Pocket Full of Stones"; 8 Ball & MJG's "Mr. Big"; and Notorious B.I.G.'s "10 Crack Commandments."

Trap music's signature sound evolved from the Southern bass music movement of the mid-1980s, California's gangsta rap of the early 1990s, the screwed-up Houston sound of the late 1990s, Memphis' underground rap scene of the late 1990s and early 2000s, and Atlanta's crunk music of the early 2000s.

Atlanta's Trap music scene can be divided into separate eras. Before Trap music became an official genre, artists such as Hitman Sammy Sam, Hard Boyz, A Damn Shame, Mr. Ku, Ghetto Mafia, and Backbone and Cool Breeze of the Dungeon Family laid a foundation with themes of street life in Atlanta.

The Trap music trinity—T.I., Young Jeezy, Gucci Mane— cultivated the first movement of the genre in the early 2000s. By the mid-2010s, Trap music proved to be a viable genre with chart-topping artists which included Migos, Future, 2 Chainz, Young Thug, 21 Savage, and producers Mike Will Made-It, Sonny Digital, 808 Mafia, and Metro Boomin. The following era that emerged in the late 2010s and early 2020s was led by Lil Baby, Gunna and others rappers from Atlanta such as Young Nudy, Trouble, Peewee Longway, Skooly, Yung Mal, Lil Keed, and Ralo, to name a few. During that period, Atlanta-based female rappers such as LightSkinKeisha, Omeretta, Akbar V, SupaPeach, and Mulatto carved their own lane within the industry.

In August 2020, Mulatto, also known as Big Latto, became the first solo female rapper from Atlanta to earn a gold plaque for her song, "Bitch from Da Souf." She would also gain national attention with her bold freestyle that was featured on *XXL* magazine's "2020 Freshman Cypher."

The sound of Trap music may vary considering the producer, but the lyrical content often remains the same. Money is the goal, drugs are the tools, the hustle is imperative, and violence can be a repercussion. Trap music is an observation of dysfunction, but it's also a celebration of what would appear to be an economic triumph.

In its essence, Trap music is black music. It derives from a city where black is bold, revolutionary, and inspiring. Trap music can express the neglect and desperation of Atlanta's inner-city youth who often feel trapped in poverty while witnessing the celebrity-driven scene of Atlanta's entertainment industry. Trap music stands as the byproduct of systemic racism, poor-performing schools, high unemployment rates, and America's ongoing war on drugs. Trap music reveals itself as the sound of young blacks feeling trapped by a lack of options and somehow viewing drugs and crime as the only way out. Trap music is the rhythm of despair, short-term success in the drug trade, and the inevitable reality of being the next victim of the ultimate trap, mass incarceration.

With this book, I explore Trap music and the Trap in three sections. In part one, I examine the beginnings of Trap music and how artists such as T.I., Gucci

Mane, and Jeezy laid the foundation for the genre. In part two, I take readers into one of the most notorious drug Traps in America and shed light on the social ills that have often inspired the content in Trap music. And in part three, I delve into the historical significance of the genre and global impact of Trap culture.

While covering music, entertainment, and politics as a journalist, I got the opportunity to interview prominent figures who played a role in crafting the genre of Trap music. During my career, I've interviewed artists such as T.I., Gucci Mane, Young Jeezy (who would be known as Jeezy later in his career), Future, Young Thug, Big Boi, Goodie Mob, Zaytoven, DJ Toomp, and DJ Drama to name a few.

I also spoke with individuals who have sold drugs, used drugs, and lived in neighborhoods that were commonly known as the Trap. To further understand the criminal repercussions of life in the Trap, I spoke with legal experts and college professors who reveal how certain laws affect drug offenders.

I analyze the global impact of Trap music through interviews with international artists who were inspired by the Atlanta-created genre.

This book is an exploration of every aspect of the Trap and reveals what it represents for music, a city, culture, internationally, and an entire generation.

(Top L-R) Shawty Lo, T.I., Gucci Mane, Jeezy, 2 Chainz, Future, Quavo of Migos, Young Thug, 21 Savage.

PART I: THE MUSIC

CHAPTER
I

WELCOME TO TRAPLANTA

City of Atlanta

With Underground Kingz' "Pocket Full of Stones" blasting from a portable boom box, 14-year-old Tee placed his video game controller on the floor and stood. He turned, walked to a closet, and grabbed a Nike shoe box. Tee removed the lid from the box and pulled out a small wad of cash held together by a rubber band. A silver-plated .22 caliber handgun and a single Ziplock bag appeared beneath the money. Tee lifted his long white T-shirt, exposing the black beeper hooked to his jeans and put the money in his pocket. He proceeded and pulled the Ziploc bag out of the shoe box. Tee opened the Ziploc bag, and I watched as small blue bags filled with tan rocks fell into the palm of his hands. I was 12-years old, and it was the first time I saw crack cocaine.

Tee was a friend who lived with his grandmother near my childhood home in the Oakland City community of southwest, Atlanta. Seeing crack cocaine in the hands of a 14-year-old friend proved that we were no longer just competing in sports and video games to pass the time. Tee was now playing a game where there were more significant repercussions for the winners and losers. The winners often made more money than most young men our age. On the other hand, the losers faced prison time, violence or death.

Crack cocaine became a topic of discussion moments earlier as Tee, and I listened to UGK's "Pocket Full of Stones." Pimp C and Bun B's first prominent rap single detailed the life of drug dealers with rags to riches ambitions. The duo's vivid wordplay took listeners to a place where drugs, sex, and souls were sold. Bun B perfectly described the allure to such evil as "the Devil's love potion." Tee and I nodded our heads to Pimp C's production on "Pocket Full of Stones," which sampled Eugene McDaniels' song "Freedom Death Dance." While I remained fully engaged in the rap lyrics which provided menacing details of crack cocaine's power, Tee took a moment to share with me how "Pocket Full of Stones" was more than just a rap song to him, it served as a soundtrack to his first occupation.

Tee revealed that his uncle would take him to a location a few blocks away from his home in Oakland City. They would stand on a corner with several other dealers for hours at a time. Tee would hand the drugs to the buyers after his uncle would receive money. At 14-years old, Tee was considered a juvenile and would not face severe prosecution if caught by the Atlanta police. Once they sold out on a package, Tee would get a cut of the money from his uncle. He said the money allowed him to help pay bills at his grandmother's house and he was also able to buy video games and new sneakers.

Tee's uncle carried the appearance and swagger of a 1980s-era dope boy. He drove a 1982 Cadillac Eldorado that featured an elaborate yellow paint job and massive speakers in the trunk. The neighborhood residents could hear him from blocks away as he blasted songs like "Life Is...Too Short" by Too $hort and N.W.A.'s "Dope Man." He dressed like the rappers we would see in music videos by wearing designer shades, clean Adidas jumpsuits, new Air Jordans and Shell Toe Adidas sneakers, and small gold chains around his neck. But he was far from a rapper. He lived the life that some rap artists glorified in songs.

Crack cocaine was the drug that put money in the pockets of some and destroyed the lives of others. It was a drug that manifested power for those who sold it and could evoke pity for those who used it. Crack cocaine was a source of prosperity and also a gateway to spending years behind bars. It helped some families pay bills while ripping other families apart.

It also became a tool for politicians looking to start a perpetual war on drugs where the enemy was often poor and black. Illegal drugs became an essential component of our environment and the music that my friends and I loved the most shed light on the ordeal.

Rap is high on drugs. So it's not a coincidence that drug use and drug abuse served as major themes in rap songs. The harsh environments wrote the songs before rappers recorded the ideas in a studio.

If crack cocaine and hip-hop helped to define an aspect of our generation, the Anti-Drug Abuse Act of 1986 and the Violent Crime Control and Law Enforcement Act of 1994 became laws that nearly destroyed it. Signed by President Ronald Reagan, the Anti-Drug Abuse Act relied on fear and racial coding that presented crack cocaine as a substance that could end civilization.

Crack cocaine was viewed as a drug that would most likely be used by poor minorities as opposed to cocaine, which cost more on the underground market. The Anti-Drug Abuse Act imposed a five-year mandatory sentence for the sale or distribution of five grams of crack cocaine. In turn, a person could sell up to five hundred grams of cocaine to receive a similar sentence.

The act created a massive increase in America's prison system. And while whites and minorities both use illegal drugs at an almost equal rate, most of the people who were incarcerated for drug crimes were black and Latino.

"When we think of drugs like crack cocaine, black people use crack about the same pace as white people," Dr. Carl Hart of Columbia University revealed to me. "Now, when you think about the fact that the federal laws are regulating cocaine, eighty-five percent of the people prosecuted are black. We place our law enforcement resources in black communities, and we go after black people. We target black people. The laws are not racist; it is our applications of the laws. It is our law enforcement. That is what is racist."

Nearly one decade after the passing of the Anti-Drug Abuse Act, President Bill Clinton signed the Violent Crime Control and Law Enforcement Act. The bill provided $9 billion for new prisons if states would reduce parole eligibility for prisoners. The law also enforced mandatory life sentences for three-time felons. So a person who was convicted twice on drug charges could spend the rest of their life behind bars if they got into a fistfight and were convicted a third time on battery charges. The law often failed to measure circumstances.

Before signing the bill, members of the Congressional Black Caucus warned Clinton and expressed why the law was racially biased. But Clinton ignored their requests and signed the bill into law. During Clinton's term as president, the nation's incarceration rate increased by sixty percent with over one million inmates being black.

With the passing of the Violent Crime Control and Law Enforcement Act and the Anti-Drug Abuse Act, the era of mass incarceration was born. The nation's prison population increased from 330,000 in 1973 to over two million by 2002. Centuries after the abolishment of slavery, America again found itself in the business of incarcerating brown bodies for profit, and arrests for drug crimes were the easiest way to feed its system.

The term Trap surfaced as a reference to drug locations in Atlanta in the early 1990s. It perfectly described the urban environments where thousands of citizens became trapped by poverty and a lack of opportunities. Nearly one-quarter of a million Atlantans were living in poverty at the start of the 1990s, and over half of those citizens were black. A majority of people who were living in poverty during that time resided in one of the fifteen thousand individual units owned by the Atlanta Housing Authority. The subsidized housing was commonly known as the projects.

Most of the projects in Atlanta featured confined spaces where drug Traps could prosper. The rows of three-story brick buildings usually formed a square around a courtyard or open area. At night, some drug dealers would shoot out the street lights surrounding the courtyard, making the area pitch-black so police would have difficulty viewing illegal activity. The dealers sold drugs to the addicts, paid some residents to stash drugs inside of apartment units, and hired lookouts who roamed the projects and informed the dealers of police presence.

The Traps that existed in the housing projects were a world within themselves. Once a crew claimed a Trap, outsiders could be met with violence if they attempted to deal drugs in that area. The Trap served as real estate, and prominent drug crews established their territories early. It proved to be a rare occasion where poor and prosperity intertwined. The neighborhoods which held the lowest home values in Atlanta were the areas where the Traps thrived the most. The city's most notorious project was Techwood Homes.

Located in downtown Atlanta near Georgia Tech and Coca-Cola's main headquarters, the U.S. government built Techwood Homes in 1935 as an answer to slum housing. Techwood Homes soon became a staple of President Franklin D. Roosevelt's New Deal and served as a national model to provide housing for the poor following the Great Depression. The nation's first housing project, Techwood initially only housed white residents as University Homes (opened in 1938), located near the Atlanta University Center, served as the first public housing to accept black residents in Atlanta. After three decades of racial segregation, Techwood Homes became a majority-black housing project following white flight during the late 1960s.

By the 1970s, the projects were places that housed the forgotten. Thousands of low-income families lived in small quarters detached from mainstream society. The housing projects were cities within a city, locations where poverty flourished and hope could easily die.

Amid the despair, some found ways to survive. With high unemployment rates, residents turned to the underground economy for income. Backroom hairstylists, street mechanics, apartment cooks, and owners of makeshift candy stores found ways to earn extra income without obtaining a business license. Poverty created restrictions, but a sense of freedom existed for some who provided a skill or product in the underground economy.

A generation of Atlanta number runners such as Julian "Q Ball" Scott and Donald "Ducky" Moore controlled the street scene of the underground economy during the 1960s and 1970s. But as the crack cocaine era emerged in the 1980s, Atlanta's housing projects and the underground economy would never be the same.

DOPE AND DEATH: STORY OF THE MIAMI BOYS

When most of the young men smiled, their gold teeth glistened. Thick gold chains hung from their necks, and a few sported Jheri curl hairstyles. In a city where professional sports teams included the Atlanta Braves, Atlanta Falcons, and Atlanta Hawks, the young men represented their hometown by wearing Starter jackets of the Miami Hurricanes and Miami Dolphins with pride. The crew of young men, most in their late teens and early 20s, were not visitors seeking to make friends. They were all from Miami, and they arrived in Atlanta to take over the drug game.

In 1986, the residents of Techwood Homes noticed the new visitors roaming their neighborhood. The Miami Boys became the first significant drug crew to infiltrate the city of Atlanta during the height of the crack cocaine era. Formed by a group of drug dealers from the Liberty City and Carol City neighborhoods in Miami, the Miami Boys operated under Miami-based drug kingpin Isaac "Big Ike" Hicks and a few other major drug suppliers in South Florida.

With Hicks having a direct connection to the Colombian drug trade which supplied some of the purest cocaine in the Southeast region, the Miami Boys would eventually expand their operation beyond South Florida. Crews that originated from South Florida began to take trips via Interstate 75 North to sell drugs in Orlando, Jacksonville, and other small towns in Florida and Georgia. The Miami Boys were able to take over and turn a profit in every city, but they discovered that Atlanta proved to be a goldmine.

Atlanta's rising population, its connection as a travel hub, and its forty-three housing projects made the city an attractive location for the Miami Boys. A more considerable profit margin for cocaine also existed in Atlanta. An ounce of cocaine that sold for $500 in Miami sold for as much as $1,800 in Atlanta. At their peak, the crew's net pay reached up to $200,000 per week. Crew leaders began to recruit and give wayward teens in Miami one-way bus or airline tickets to Atlanta.

"Guys took the Miami game and went to Atlanta with it," James Sawyer, former Miami Boys member and author of the book, *The Original Miami Boys*, told me during an interview in 2019. "Everyone couldn't hustle in Miami. It was too much competition. But they could double their money in Atlanta. People in Atlanta never saw that kind of game before. It was so powerful."

Within two years of the Miami Boys' entrance into Atlanta, arrest for juvenile offenders, age 17-years-old and under, tripled. The Miami Boys saw that Atlanta was ripe for the drug trade and entered the city with brute force. Their weapons of choice were UZIs, MAC 10s, and Florida-made 9mm machine guns.

"The Miami Boys set the standard for what a drug gang was supposed to be," John Turner, who served as Assistant District Attorney in Fulton County during the 1980s, shared with me. "My initial impression of them was that they were extremely violent and didn't hesitate to kill."

The Miami Boys set up shop in several Atlanta area projects in 1986. Along with Techwood Homes, the Miami Boys also operated in other housing projects such as John Hope Homes and University Homes.

"Places like Techwood and Perry homes were relatively large areas with dense concentration," Turner said. "So you had a situation where [the housing projects] were, in some regards, isolated. You also had a place where customers knew where to come and make their purchases, and you had a perfect distribution system if you wanted to be a drug dealer. The Miami Boys seized on that, and that was the nature of the problem."

The Miami Boys figured out the independent drug dealers who sold in those areas and forced them to either work for them or face consequences that could be fatal.

Ronald Baker, a 22-year-old resident of Techwood Homes, began earning a reputation as one of the top dealers in the projects in the mid-1980s. When members of the Miami Boys arrived in Atlanta in 1986, they wanted Baker's territory and warned him against selling drugs in Techwood. However, Baker ignored their threats and remained true to his operation. He continued to sell drugs in Techwood, and the Miami Boys sent a vicious message to prove a point.

Several months after they initially arrived in Atlanta, members of the Miami Boys reportedly kidnapped Baker. Days after being reported missing, Baker was found in a suburb of Atlanta (Gwinnett County) with several bullet holes in his head. His lifeless body had been dumped on the side of the road. Police viewed members of the Miami Boys as the prime suspects.

The Miami Boys were also suspects in another case where an independent dealer was shot twelve times while standing on a corner in Techwood. Within a year of operating in Atlanta, the Miami Boys were linked to thirteen homicides by local police.

"The first substantial case I had involving a member of the Miami Boys was with an individual who committed several murders," Turner recalled. "What was unique about that situation was that it was the first time the RICO law was used in Fulton County because it had been so relatively new. He was convicted and got a life sentence. Word came back that I had been threatened by him and other members. I remember talking to the district attorney about it. I just figured it was the cost of doing business."

The Miami Boys' aggression led to their downfall. On a fall evening one year following Baker's death, 60-year-old Emma Louis Johnson was sitting on her porch in University Homes when violence erupted. The Miami Boys were attempting to intimidate an equally powerful crew led by an Atlanta dealer, Terry White. During a gun battle between the Miami Boys and Terry White's crew, Emma Louis Johnson was murdered in the place she called home.

Johnson's death sparked community outrage, and Atlanta officials were pressured to put an end to the violence caused by some drug crews. In 1987, 207 homicides were recorded in the city of Atlanta. The violence furthered the rift between white residents in the metro area who accused Mayor Andrew Young of being soft on violence. They often claimed that the city's black leadership failed to make downtown Atlanta safe for shopping, entertainment, and tourism.

Public Safety Commissioner George Napper responded by creating a unit that, in theory, would rival the aggression of drug organizations that mostly operated in public housing communities. Napper and police Major Eldrin Bell unleashed the Red Dogs (Run Every Drug Dealer Out of Georgia) into the streets of Atlanta. The Red Dogs were a police unit formed to counter the street-level drug dealers and violence. Before the Red Dogs were formed, drug calls were often handled by a few officers on the Atlanta Police Department. Napper, a football fan, admired the "red-dog" blitz play where teams would rush six defenders at the quarterback, forcing him to either make a quick throw, run, or be sacked. The Red Dogs mirrored that aggression. The special unit consisted of twenty-five to thirty police officers who were physically built like middle linebackers.

The officers entered drug-infested areas, aggressively raiding Trap houses and arresting suspected drug dealers. Within a year on the streets, the Red Dogs were averaging six hundred arrests per month. At times, the Red Dogs' tactics often tread the line between toughness and police brutality. That same brutality would put the unit in jeopardy two decades later.

Along with the Red Dogs, the Miami Boys also became targets of a crew who called themselves the International Robbing Crew. The Robbing Crew witnessed the massive amounts of money the Miami Boys earned and set up plans to rob the dealers and, at times, the stash where they would keep their profits and drugs. Stealing from drug dealers proved to be the perfect crime when executed correctly. It became a theft that could never be reported to the police. The only form of justice would be retaliation.

Tony Minter, a man who resided in Herndon Homes, allegedly robbed several of the Miami Boys' street-level drug dealers. On July 31, 1990, two members of the Miami Boys approached Minter and reportedly shot him and two other bystanders on an outdoor basketball court. A third member of the Miami Boys waited in a car and served as the getaway driver during the retaliation. Six months later, three members of the

Miami Boys were convicted of Minter's murder and another retaliation death. They were all sentenced to life in prison.

A few years after the Miami Boys took over the most lucrative drug Traps in Atlanta, their crew began to fall apart slowly. Murder convictions, the arrests of street-level dealers by Red Dog police officers, and the Robbing Crew's intense pressure on rival crew members disrupted the Miami Boys' operation in Atlanta.

Back in Miami, police raided a home allegedly owned by "Big Ike" Hicks in 1987 and seized twenty-four pounds of cocaine and over $500,000 in cash and jewelry. Hicks was sentenced to one hundred and thirty-seven years in prison but died several years later due to an illness while in jail. Another prominent leader of the Miami Boys, Winston Theodore Brown, was sentenced to thirty years in prison on racketeering charges and for a murder that occurred in Techwood Homes in 1988. But while the drug arrests, murder convictions, and the Robbing Crew were disruptions to the Miami Boys, the crew could not survive without a Trap.

When most of the Miami Boys were kids, there was an initial plan to destroy Techwood Homes. In 1974, Coca-Cola's president J. Paul Austin wanted to demolish the housing project. With Coca-Cola headquarters only one block away, Austin feared that the rising black population and crime in Techwood would hinder his company's business.

In an attempt to solve what he viewed as a problem, Austin proposed a plan with architect John Portman to remove Techwood Homes, relocate its residents, and build a business complex and retail spaces. The plan was close to being implemented until Mayor Maynard Jackson went against the idea once the news media published the details of the proposed deal. Jackson, Atlanta's first black mayor, did not want to be viewed as a leader who allowed a corporate power to displace hundreds of black residents who resided in low-income housing. Jackson would not allow Techwood Homes to be destroyed by Austin and Coca-Cola in the 1970s, but he could not save the housing projects once Atlanta prepared to host the biggest sporting event in the city's history.

The plan that Austin presented two decades earlier to replace Techwood Homes suddenly became more appealing to city leaders in 1990. Along with Techwood, the Atlanta Housing Authority began implementing an initiative to demolish a majority of public housing in the city. The political ploy got rid of dilapidated housing and moved the poor out of the city before Atlanta captured the world's attention. Most of the inner-city projects were replaced by mixed-income housing. The new mixed-income homes were often too expensive for many of the residents who relied on federal assistance.

Once the International Olympic Committee announced in 1990 that Atlanta would serve as host of the 1996 Olympics, it felt like a significant victory for a city that had yet to win a Super Bowl, World Series, or NBA Finals. Once nicknamed "Loserville" by *Sports Illustrated*, the city of Atlanta suffered for decades when it came to sports. Somehow, the Olympics was supposed to undo years of pathetic sports play and give residents the feeling of being winners. But if the city won an opportunity to host the Olympic games, poor blacks were the losers.

Bulldozers arrived in Techwood Homes to demolish each unit several months before the Olympic torch was lit by the great Muhammad Ali to open the 1996 Olympic Games. In case there were any misconceptions, the demolishing of Techwood Homes proved how poor blacks were still disposable in a city that claimed to embrace blackness. Even in a city where blacks held high positions of leadership, the concerns of poor minorities were ignored. A majority of the residents who were displaced were forced to relocate to apartments twenty or more miles away from the city's epicenter. City leaders argued that the removal of Techwood Homes and other housing projects would reduce crime. But that bandage could only cover the city's wounds for so long.

As Techwood Homes crumbled to the ground with the help of bulldozers, so did the power of the Miami Boys. With the multiple convictions of their top crew members, the Miami Boys' dominance on the streets of Atlanta came to an end. By the opening ceremony of the 1996 Olympics, the Miami Boys were an afterthought.

Dismantling the housing projects and the Miami Boys did little to eradicate the city's crime and drug trade. New drug dealers learned the game and established their own drug Traps in different locations around the city of Atlanta.

CHAPTER II

HOW STRIP CLUB CULTURE
&
BASS MUSIC
GAVE RISE TO
SOUTHERN RAP

Magic City.

With a mix of Atlanta-based rap music blasting from speakers, nude women danced in front of a man who reclined in the VIP section of a dimly-lit club. Dressed like a platinum-selling rapper with a diamond cuban link around his neck, gold-framed sunglasses over his eyes, and an iced-out grill on his teeth, the man's stretched hands could barely grip the stack of dollar bills he held in the air. A few more nude women emerged from the dressing room and offered to entertain several clean-cut men dressed in business attire who were seated at the bar. On the opposite end of the club, a group of young men, dressed in hoodies and T-shirts, sat near a group of women who partook in meals prepared in the club's kitchen. Another nude woman danced near them. The day had just begun; it was lunchtime at Magic City.

Since opening with one exotic dancer in 1985 on Forsyth Street in downtown Atlanta, Magic City has become one of the most recognized strip clubs in America. The strip club, also known for its exceptional chicken wings, stands as a landmark along with another prominent Atlanta strip club, Blue Flame Lounge. Similar to visiting the National Mall while in Washington, D.C., walking through the French Quarters while in New Orleans, or eating a cheesesteak while in Philadelphia, partying at an Atlanta strip club became a necessity for many adults who traveled to the city. The top strip clubs in Atlanta are not grungy spots where creepy old men go to look at college-aged women; they are where fantasy and the city's intriguing music industry intersect.

Strip clubs played a significant role in establishing Atlanta's rap scene. In the early days of rap, national radio and TV outlets often marginalized Southern rappers. Besides Scarface and the Geto Boys and, at times, Luther Campbell's 2 Live Crew, music video shows on BET and MTV primarily showcased rappers who hailed from New York and California.

From a local standpoint, V-103 stood as the top urban FM radio station in Atlanta during the 1980s and only played rap music on Friday nights with a show called "The Fresh Party." Radio personality Greg Street would bring a hip-hop edge to V-103 when he joined the station in June 1995. And Radio One would also enter the Atlanta market with the all-rap radio station HOT 97.5 in 1995 as well. Ludacris, known then as "Chris Lova Lova," and La La Vazquez-Anthony would co-host the "Future Flavas" show on HOT 97.5.

Arnell Starr, a local video jockey, provided a platform for Atlanta rappers with his one-hour music video show, "American Music Makers," which aired on a local TV station on Saturday nights.

In the late 1990s, Munson Steed published *Rolling Out* magazine which gave an editorial voice to Atlanta's music scene while also providing job opportunities for graduates of HBCUs and metro-area colleges.

Atlanta still remained behind the media reach of New York and L.A., so most Atlanta-based rappers realized their best chance for initial exposure came by way of strippers and strip club DJs. In the 1980s, strip clubs, and at times skating rinks, were the only outlets for aspiring rappers from Atlanta.

"The strip clubs and rappers both benefited from each other," Michael Barney, founder of Magic City, shared with me. "Hip-hop took it and blew life into the stripping game. The rappers played a big part in keeping the strip club culture alive. Videos gave strippers a whole new avenue. I don't think it would be anything close to what it turned out to be without hip-hop. On the other hand, local rappers were able to benefit by getting exposure in the club."

The early days of Atlanta's strip club culture coincided with the beginning of a subgenre of rap music that embraced booty shaking and bass. Known as bass music, it became the first subgenre of rap to emerge from the South.

Initially established in Miami and finding a second home in Atlanta, bass music merged the hard-thumping sounds of African Bambaataa's "Don't Stop...Planet Rock," with chants and repetitive hooks that were backed by up-tempo 808 drums and synthesizers.

M.C. A.D.E.'s "Bass Rock Express" was credited as the first Miami bass song and 2 Live Crew's "Throw the 'D'" helped to solidify the bass music sound in 1986. Atlanta native DJ Toomp toured with 2 Live Crew when he was a teenager and helped to bring the sound to Atlanta by producing for Atlanta-based rappers MC Shy D and Raheem The Dream.

"We were making what some people called booty-shaking music," DJ Toomp shared. "A lot of the songs were about booty shaking. Songs like 'Shake Whatcha Mama Gave Ya' and 'Move Something' was about girls and dancing. Bass music changed the city [of Atlanta]. Some people say in a bad way, but I think it changed it in a good way. We needed a melting pot of black folks from different regions."

With a focus on party and dance, most of Atlanta's bass music did not reflect how the war on drugs affected the city. The music played in the strip clubs and skating rinks were mostly dance-heavy and sex-driven. But there were a few bass music artists who dared to share a glimpse of Atlanta's drug culture.

Kilo Ali mastered the bass music sound by adding melody and a bit of lyricism to his songs. His first rap single, released in 1990, provided an insightful look at Atlanta's drug epidemic.

Kilo Ali wrote "Cocaine (America Has a Problem)" as a 16-year-old while doing a stint at the Fulton County Juvenile Detention Center. He was arrested and charged after shooting an older man who punched him during a confrontation in the Bowen Homes housing projects. Once released from juvenile (the man he shot lived), Kilo Ali recorded the song at Soundscape Studios in 1988. Soundscape Studios would become a staple of Atlanta's music scene after it was acquired by Bobby Brown in 1991 and later bought by OutKast, who transformed it to Stankonia Studios in 1999.

"Cocaine (America Has a Problem)" combined the uptempo production of bass music with a rap that delved into drug addiction, power, and incarceration.

Kilo Ali presented a fatal love story where the drug user and drug dealer both covet a "white girl" named cocaine. The "white girl" changed lives, allowed poor youth to earn money and buy new clothes, cars, gold chains, and a home. But like any unstable relationship, the good times would not last. The dealer killed to maintain the "white girl" and the power it brings. The song ends with the drug dealer being arrested by police as the "white girl" finds its way back to the streets, ensuring that the cycle of drug addiction and violence continues.

"It wasn't about selling cocaine, it wasn't about doing cocaine, it was about the person in the middle of the Trap who sees it all," Kilo Ali told me during an interview three decades after the songs' initial release. "My uncle comes and steals my grandmother's TV to do crack, and my cousin sells the crack. So I gave a three-dimensional story so people can see it from all around the bases."

The success of "Cocaine (America Has a Problem)" appeared to be the perfect beginning to a promising career for Kilo Ali. Before OutKast, T.I., Jeezy, or Gucci Mane, Kilo Ali was the undisputed king of Atlanta rap. Kilo made songs for the strip clubs, "Nasty Dancer"; he made songs for the skating rinks, "Show Me Love"; he even made a few conscious rap songs, "Lost Y'all Mind." When Kilo Ali released a new project, most Atlanta-area teens would rush to local record stores to buy the album, cassette, or CD.

But Kilo found very little success outside of Atlanta and the Southern region. He came close to experiencing mainstream success after signing with production trio Organized Noize. In 1997, Organized Noize signed a distribution deal with Interscope Records and gave Kilo Ali his first major record label release with the album, *Organized Bass*. The album included a song tailor-made for radio, the Prince-inspired "Baby, Baby." *Organized Bass* also included a collaboration with Big Boi of OutKast for the raunchy, yet sonically appealing, "Love in Ya Mouth." Both songs were regional hits that never caught on in mainstream markets such as New York and Los Angeles.

Due to creative differences with Interscope, Organized Noize would eventually walk away from their $20 million distribution deal, reportedly leaving $17 million on the table.

Kilo Ali faced struggles of his own. While dealing with drug addiction, he was sentenced to fifteen years in prison after being convicted of burning down his own house in 2005. He served six years of that sentence and was released in January of 2011. By the time of his release, the entire rap game changed and his best days as a rapper appeared to be in the past. However, Kilo's influence remained. Every Atlanta rap artist who found success owes a nod to Kilo Ali. "Cocaine (America Has a Problem)" was a precursor to Trap music.

Kilo Ali would give the nod to another artist who came of age on Atlanta's rap scene in the 1980s. He shared with me his thoughts on why Hitman Sammy Sam should be considered the first Trap music artist from Atlanta.

"If everyone could do their research, they'll know that Sammy Sam was the first Trap rapper from Atlanta," Kilo told me "It's no doubt about it. He was the first Trap star out of Atlanta."

The life Hitman Sammy Sam led on the streets of Atlanta often overshadowed his music. He served multiple stints in prison and was shot fifteen times. But when focused on music, Hitman Sammy Sam could create anthems.

Hitman Sammy Sam's 1988 song, "The Hitman," gave fans of rap music the first glimpse of Atlanta's street life. In 1998, Sammy Sam would sign with Big Oomp Records, an indpendent label and record store franchise based in southwest, Atlanta. Sammy Sam released songs that resonated in Atlanta nightclubs such as "Knuckle Up" and "Intoxicated." His biggest hit came in 2003 after signing a joint venture deal with Universal Records for the comical song, "Step Daddy." But it was his first song in 1988, "The Hitman," which could arguably be Atlanta's first hardcore rap song.

Another song that predated Trap music was Success-N-Effect's 1989 single, "Roll It Up My N—."

Along with Kilo Ali, Hitman Sammy Sam, and Success-N-Effect, several other local rap acts revealed how the drug epidemic had an impact on Atlanta during the 1980s and 1990s. Artists such as The Hard Boys, Ghetto Mafia, CMP (Causing Much Pain), and A-Dam-Shame released songs that contained elements of Trap music years before it became a genre.

Bass music, strip club culture, and the war on drugs were elements that influenced and shaped the beginnings of Southern rap in the 1980s—a form of rap that would have a major impact on music in the decades to come.

CHAPTER III

OUTKAST, THE ERA OF CRUNK, AND ATLANTA'S EPIC NIGHTLIFE

OutKast. André 3000/Big Boi

Hours before twenty-thousand people filled the grounds of Centennial Olympic Park for the "ATLast" festival, a buzz of excitement resonated in downtown Atlanta on the final weekend of September 2014. Shortly after nightfall, a black curtain lifted, revealing Big Boi and André 3000 together on stage in Atlanta for the first time in nearly a decade. Following the release of the 2006 album *Idlewild*, the duo would take a hiatus from recording as a group which caused their fans to yearn for a return. The deafening roar of twenty-thousand was that of a city claiming greatness and owning its new identity as the capital of urban music.

The ATLast festival proved to be a victory lap for OutKast that made every native of Atlanta proud. We were proud of the duo who gave the world a dose of our city through song, and in turn, a glimpse of who we are and what we can become.

Atlanta's music scene can be divided into two eras: B.O. (Before OutKast) and A.O. (After OutKast). Before OutKast hit the music scene in the early 1990s, Atlanta was culturally a forgotten city. In hip-hop, New York was the Mecca. Los Angeles and Compton always seemed close to the crown and, arguably, held it for some years.

And other cities such as Houston, Bay Area, Chicago, and Miami all made listeners pay attention to their perspectives in hip-hop. Before OutKast, Atlanta's music scene was similar to the ballplayers who could hear the game from outside of the stadium, but never allowed the opportunity to go inside and play on the field.

Atlanta's early hip-hop never escaped the barrier of Interstate 285. Kilo Ali, Raheem The Dream and Hitman Sammy Sam were legends from Bankhead to Campbellton Road. But fans of rap who resided in California or New York could never relate to the feeling of hearing Kilo Ali's "Hear What I Hear" while roller skating at Jelly Beans or Screaming Wheels on a Saturday night. Atlanta always had something to say, even when it seemed as if we were the only ones listening. OutKast forced the nation to finally pay attention.

André "Dre" Benjamin, later known as André 3000, and Antwan "Big Boi" Patton met in the early 1990s while students at Tri-Cities High School, a school located in East Point, Georgia. Initially known as 2 Shades Deep, the teen duo would get their big break after meeting Rico Wade who was a member of the production trio, Organized Noize. In 1991, Wade held a job as a manager at Lamonte's Beauty Supply store in East Point when Dre and Big Boi arrived at the store's parking lot to showcase their rap skills. Big Gipp, who would become a member of the rap group Goodie Mob, blasted A Tribe Called Quest's "Scenario" from the speakers of his car as Dre and Big Boi rapped for nearly ten minutes straight. Thoroughly impressed by their lyricism and delivery, Wade invited Dre and Big Boi to the Dungeon, a makeshift studio located in the basement of Wade's mother's home.

The Dungeon served as the creative space for Organized Noize (Wade, Sleepy Brown, and Ray Murray) to craft music for OutKast and artists such as Goodie Mob, Cool Breeze, Backbone, EJ The Witchdoctor, Big Rube, and Parental Advisory. The collective would be known as the Dungeon Family.

While the Dungeon Family worked on honing their skills in a basement, L.A. Reid and Babyface relocated to Atlanta to start their label, LaFace Records. With backing by Clive Davis' Arista Records and BMG Entertainment, LaFace had access to the one thing that most Atlanta-based record labels lacked at the time—worldwide distribution. Initially, a label that focused on pop and R&B music, L.A. Reid would give OutKast an opportunity by first placing them on the remix to TLC's "What About Your Friends" and giving them a song placement on LaFace's Christmas album, *A LaFace Family Christmas*. That song became OutKast's first major single, "Player's Ball."

When OutKast released "Player's Ball" on November 19, 1993, Atlanta was born again. The city became another place. There was a new energy, a new vibe, a new approach to culture. Imagine being present when Langston Hughes, Zora Neale Hurston, and Paul Robeson were crafting their first pieces of work in what would become the Harlem Renaissance. OutKast's "Player's Ball" gave rise to Atlanta's rap renaissance.

This time, the music felt different. They were telling our story. The kids of Atlanta finally had a voice in hip-hop. OutKast would inherently express the stories of a city through music.

OutKast possessed the lyricism of New York emcees while being able to flow over beats like rappers from the West Coast. They could represent the pimp/player motif similar to Memphis, Tennessee's 8Ball & MJG, and Port Arthur, Texas' UGK. And they were also as eclectic as New York's A Tribe Called Quest and California's Hieroglyphics. OutKast delivered rap verses through thick Southern accents that embodied our reality of being young, black, and from Atlanta. The group did not seek to appease other regions that, at the time, had a stronghold on rap. OutKast introduced the rap industry to Atlanta and, in a sense, the rap industry would eventually become Atlanta.

"I remember life in Atlanta before OutKast, and it's nothing like it is now," T.I. shared with me during an interview. "Although we appreciate Sammy Sam, MC Shy D, and Kilo Ali, until OutKast, So So Def, and LaFace came, we weren't recognized and appreciated abroad like we are now. I believe they got it here."

Quavo of Migos also shared his thoughts on OutKast's impact on rap. "Atlanta builds and creates when it comes to music," Quavo said during an interview in 2016. "We come from the North Side and Atlanta embraced us as the young wave and young creators. I feel like they created us and we're just keeping it going. Atlanta has always been creative. The city became what it is because of legends like OutKast."

OutKast would prove their greatness over the decades after initially being shunned by New Yorkers. During the infamous Source Awards on the night of August 3, 1995, OutKast endured heckles and boos at the Madison Square Garden Paramount Theater. The ceremony amplified the bicoastal rap beef between Death Row Records and Bad Boy Entertainment and OutKast were likely victims of the intensity in the room that night. Following their win for the Best New Artist of the Year award, Dre challenged the rowdy New York crowd with the declaration, "The South got something to say!"

In the years following that night in 1995, the South would say and do a lot on its way to dominating every aspect of rap.

THE RAPPER WHO INTRODUCED THE WORD TRAP TO MUSIC

Following the success of OutKast, Organized Noize and LaFace Records would introduce Goodie Mob. Khujo, CeeLo Green, Big Gipp, and T-Mo stood as a four-man rap crew from southwest, Atlanta that was soulful, thought-provoking, and as inspiring as the Civil Rights leaders who made an impact in the city decades before the rise of rap music. On November 7, 1995, Goodie Mob would release their debut project *Soul Food*, which firmly addressed elements of Georgia's racist past and present, the disconnect between the city's leadership and black youth, self-empowerment, spirituality, and Atlanta's changing landscape as the 1996 Olympics approached. *Soul Food* was also the album where Dungeon Family rapper Cool Breeze introduced the term "Dirty South," which became the brand name for a region that previously lacked an identity in hip-hop.

The song "Dirty South" gave listeners a glimpse into the grimy aspects of Atlanta's street life and the last days of the Techwood Homes dope boys and Red Dog police unit. On the contemplative song, "Thought Process," which featured a guest verse from André, Khujo provided a subtle introduction to the term "Trap." It was the first time the slang term had ever been used on a mainstream rap record.

"We started recording the *Soul Food* album in 1994," Khujo Goodie shared with me. "That was my first freestyle back when I was in the Trap. While we were sitting in the Trap, my big homie said 'We're the Goodie Mob, and we're selling goodies,' which was crack cocaine at the time. When we hooked up with CeeLo [Green], that name evolved. It became an acronym for, 'the Good Die Mostly Over Bullshit.' And you take one "o" away and it stands for 'God is in every man of blackness.' At the end of the day, what are you trapping? Are you trapping product that will help your people, or are you trapping product that will hurt your people? Most trappers are trapping death to their people. I don't really know any retired trappers who are glorifying it. If you're a trapper, you should know how to come out of the Trap."

One year after Khujo became the first person to say the word "Trap" on a record, Big Boi mentioned the term "Trap" on the song "Wheelz of Steel" from OutKast's sophomore album, *ATLiens*. Big Boi would later go more in-depth into Trap and how it ultimately impacts families.

In the song "SpottieOttieDopaliscious" from the *Aquemini* album, Big Boi used spoken word to describe a tale of a young father who attempts to provide for his kids by seeking employment at UPS and the United States Postal Service. Due to a failed drug test, the young father is virtually unemployable. Without many options to earn income, the young father finds himself trapped, back in the Trap selling drugs. In Big Boi's slice of life, rewards don't exist in the Trap. Instead, it's the last resort in an attempt to maneuver out of a desperate situation.

"It's literally that, a Trap," Big Boi told me during an interview. "It is set up for you to lose. It's a game of chance. So you gotta get in and get out. You can't do it forever. You always have to have that second avenue. That second stage or phase of whatever your hustle is for you to proceed. And the smart guys know that."

OutKast and Goodie Mob introduced the word Trap to mainstream hip-hop. But before Trap music would take off, another genre of rap would emerge from the city of Atlanta.

CRUNK IN YOUR SYSTEM

The success of OutKast and Goodie Mob coincided with an emerging R&B movement in Atlanta which featured artists such as Usher, TLC, Toni Braxton, 112, Monica, Xscape, and Jagged Edge. Along with the music, Atlanta became known as a place where you could be young, black, and experience the best parties of your life. And there was no more celebrated party than Freaknik.

Freaknik laid the foundation of Atlanta being a preeminent city of partying for young blacks. The annual spring break event began in 1983 when a group of students from the Atlanta University Center met at John H. White Park on Cascade Road to eat, drink, and listen to music. Rick James' "Super Freak" was a popular song at the time, so event organizers used elements of the song's title and combined it with the word, picnic. What began as a small gathering of HBCU students eventually became the biggest block party in America. Ten years after the first small gathering at John H. White Park, Freaknik became a city-wide party that attracted over 200,000 attendees.

College-aged women and men gathered in places such as Greenbriar Mall, Underground Atlanta, Lenox Square Mall, and Piedmont Park. When they could not reach their destination due to bumper-to-bumper traffic, they took the party to the streets. The traffic jams became an opportunity for attendees to hang out of car windows and dance in the middle of the street. Popular artists at the time such as Snoop Dogg, Queen Latifah, Luther "Uncle Luke" Campbell, and Boyz II Men all attended Freaknik 1994 as BET, and MTV News provided national TV coverage. If you were young and black in the early 1990s, you made it a point to attend Freaknik, or you found yourself upset that you missed the biggest party of that era.

By 1995, we witnessed the beginning of the end of Freaknik. The city of Atlanta was one year away from hosting the summer Olympics, and some were viewing Freaknik as a nuisance. Racial dynamics also played a role. Pressured by wealthier residents in North Atlanta and the business community, Mayor Bill Campbell set in motion a plan to eradicate the soul of Freaknik.

Months before Freaknik 1996, a memo was reportedly sent to HBCUs to discourage students from coming to Atlanta. Local media highlighted incidents of crime that shed a negative light on the event and added to the backlash. For the college students who decided to visit Atlanta in the spring of 1996, they were met by over one thousand police officers who used strict tactics to control the massive crowds. Officers diverted traffic in a way that frustrated drivers and discouraged attendees from traveling to certain areas. Over the next three years, the implementation of "no cruising" zones and hundreds of citations and arrests caused partygoers to face reality. City officials in Atlanta no longer welcomed Freaknik. Freaknik's total demise became evident by 1999.

However, something more significant was born. The annual party played a major role in influencing thousands of college-educated and upwardly mobile blacks from across the nation to move to Atlanta. In his 2017 book *Higher is Waiting*, Tyler Perry revealed how visiting Atlanta to attend Freaknik led to him relocating to the city from Louisiana. Amid the days and nights of nonstop partying, Perry saw black people who had political and financial power for the first time in his life.

In 2019, Perry would open the largest film studio in America with the Tyler Perry Studios. The 330-acre property was once a Confederate army base known as Fort. McPherson and sits near the predominantly black communities of Lakewood, Oakland City, and West End. I spoke with Perry about the significance the opening and how it can inspire the next generation.

"What I want them to do, especially about being here in this neighborhood, is to see that it's tangible," Perry said during our interview. "You can touch it, because something about exposure once you see it, you realize that could really happen. And that's the thing that I want people to get. If you could just see it, touch it and feel it, you know that you can do it too."

Freaknik showed people across the nation that Atlanta was a black city where black people and black culture could thrive. City officials shut Freaknik down, but they never killed the vibe, the parties eventually moved to the nightclubs.

Atlanta's nightlife picked up where Freaknik left off at clubs such as Club Kaya, Club 112, and the Buckhead Village party district. All located in Midtown or Buckhead, those clubs were the spots where notable rappers, professional athletes, and movie stars would party when they visited Atlanta. Club 112 stood as a national treasure considering that it remained open on weekends until 6:30 a.m., as referenced by Jermaine Dupri on his 2001 song with Ludacris, "Welcome to Atlanta." Epic nights occurred at Club 112, Buckhead Village party district, and Club Kaya and its "Old School Sundays" with DJ Nabs who would often bring in big-name guests such as Jay-Z and Lauryn Hill.

But on the other side of town, the nightclubs that existed in the black communities featured an entirely different energy.

Similar to the juke joints that existed in the South decades earlier, "hood clubs" often provided the best mix of music that represented the essence of specific neighborhoods in Atlanta. During the 1990s and early 2000s, the most known clubs in Atlanta's black neighborhoods were 559 (West End); Club Silver Fox (Simpson Road); Charles Disco (Simpson Road); My Brother's Keeper (Campbellton Road); Shyran's Showcase (Gresham Road); and The Bounce (Bankhead). Ludacris would film the video for his raucous hit, "Move Bitch" at The Bounce.

Inside of The Bounce, the vibrations of booming

808 drums and snare kicks blasted from speakers in a club packed from wall-to-wall. The DJs played the best Southern hip-hop of the early 2000s— the era of Juvenile and the Hot Boys, Master P, UGK, 8 Ball & MJG, Project Pat, and Three Six Mafia. But even with good music, spirits, and women, there was always a threat that violence could erupt at any moment.

But the prospect of danger never deterred us. We knew that a small misunderstanding could lead to a straight out brawl when the combination of alcohol, dim lights, lousy security, and loud music was present. This ritual occurred every weekend. Nothing was more exciting than being on our side of town on a Saturday night, partying with our people, and listening to our music. Intensity and aggression filled the atmosphere at nightclubs such as The Bounce, 559, Club Silver Fox, and Charles Disco. The music reflected that same intensity and aggression in what became the era of crunk.

THE KING OF CRUNK

Jermaine Dupri was raised by the music industry. His father, Michael Mauldin, was a prominent music executive and Dupri served as a dancer for the rap group Whodini as a teen. Dupri had a knack for molding new acts, producing hit songs, and turning ordinary artists into superstars. When starting his record label, So So Def, Dupri wanted someone who knew the streets of Atlanta and the pulse of the city's music scene. He found that person in Lil Jon.

Lil Jon, whose real name is Jonathan Smith, could move crowds through music. A product of the Westside of Atlanta and former band member at Douglass High School, Lil Jon became a known figure in the city during the early 1990s when he would do DJ sets at different nightclubs. Dupri hired Lil Jon to work as an A&R for So So Def records, although Lil Jon did not initially understand the duties of an A&R. Once Lil Jon settled into his role at So So Def, he decided to take the music of old Atlanta and introduce it to the nation. With the backing of a major record label, Lil Jon could finally give Atlanta's bass music scene a national look that it missed during the 1980s. In the summer of 1996, So So Def released the album, *So So Def Bass All-Stars Compilation*.

Lil Jon served as the executive producer of the album which featured songs by bass music legends Edward J, Raheem The Dream, MC Shy D, Playa Puncho, and DJ Smurf. The gem of the album proved to be "My Boo" by Ghost Town DJ's, a love song with vocals by R&B artist Virgo over bass music production by Lil Jon and Rodney Perry. The track highlighted a style of mixing made famous by club DJs on Atlanta's Westside. The DJs would mix traditional R&B songs with bass music production. The a cappella vocals from songs such as Keith Sweat's "Make It Last Forever" and Shai's "If I Ever Fall in Love" were backed by sped up 808 bass kicks.

"My Boo" maintained the traditions of bass music while being palatable for mainstream radio. In 2016, the song resurfaced as a viral hit after New Jersey teens Kevin Vincent and Jeremiah Hall recreated the Running Man dance while playing "My Boo" in the background. The viral sensation allowed "My Boo" to crack the Hot 100 Billboard charts 20 years after its initial release.

Back in 1996, *So So Def Bass All-Stars Compilation* became the album that gave Lil Jon a significant name in hip-hop. One year later, Lil Jon would team up with The East Side Boyz and introduce crunk music with the album, *Get Crunk, Who U Wit: Da Album*.

Crunk music took the elements of bass music and infused it with aggressive production and repetitive hooks and chants. Credit can also be given to Memphis' "Get Buck" (bucking the system) movement made popular by Three 6 Mafia's "Tear Da Club Up." Crunk music became the soundtrack for the excitement and brutality that many experienced while partying in a Southern nightclub. The chants expressed in crunk music were battle cries for neighborhood crews who would represent their zone, city, or state.

In 1999, Pastor Troy released a symbolic ode to the state of Georgia with the vigorous "No Mo Play in G.A." Troy's declaration proved that Southern rap artists were no longer asking for respect from New York or Los Angeles anymore—they were prepared to take it. That attitude permeated throughout the state as "No Mo Play in G.A." became an anthem for Atlanta's impending takeover of hip-hop.

Archie Eversole's "We Ready"; Drama's "Left, Right"; and Baby D's "Eastside vs. Westside" were popular crunk songs that would cause instant chaos when DJs played them at nightclubs in Atlanta during the early 2000s.

Dozens of artists and independent labels such as Big Oomp Records and Raheem The Dream's Tight 2 Def Music would add to the potency of crunk music. But Lil Jon would own the era. His 2002 album with The East Side Boyz, *Kings of Crunk*, allowed him to solidify himself as a force in rap and legitimized crunk music to the mainstream. The 19-song album featured an array of artists who rapped over Lil Jon's crunk beats as he chanted on the hooks and yelled ad-libs. The album's driving force was the Ying Yang Twins-assisted, "Get Low," which reached No. 2 on the Billboard Hot 100 chart and No. 1 on Billboard's Hot Rap Tracks chart. With the release of *Crunk Juice* in 2004, Lil Jon would transition from just being another Atlanta rapper/DJ to becoming a cultural icon. His celebrity status reached a new level with an appearance on Dave Chappelle's "Chappelle Show" in the two skits titled, "A Moment in the Life of Lil Jon."

On the music front, he cornered the market when it came to party anthems, and major record labels took notice. Lil Jon monopolized urban and pop radio in 2004 with his signature sound of 808 drums and striking synths. His collaboration with Usher and Ludacris on "Lovers and Friends" prove that crunk and R&B where a perfect match. Artists from outside of Atlanta such as Janet Jackson, Nas, Ice Cube, Snoop Dogg, E-40, Fat Joe, and Mobb Deep all went against their traditional sounds to sing or rap over Lil Jon's crunk beats. His production work with Atlanta-based artists added to the city's mystique. Ciara's "Goodies," YoungBloodz' "Damn," and Usher's "Yeah!" were career-changing hits produced by Lil Jon.

The launch of BME Recordings (Black Market Entertainment) allowed Lil Jon to open doors for a new generation of crunk music artists such as Lil Scrappy ("Money in the Bank," "Forever I Love Atlanta"); Trillville ("Some Cut"); and Crime Mob ("Knuck if You Buck").

Crunk reached heights that no one imagined by starting in small clubs on the Westside of Atlanta to being cultivated into a sound by Lil Jon. The term "crunk" became so popular that it entered the Merriam-Webster Collegiate Dictionary in 2007.

By that year, crunk music had already seen its best days. But before the ascension of Trap music, another subgenre of rap would emerge on Atlanta's Westside.

CHAPTER
IV

FROM SNAP TO TRAP: THE LIFE AND TIMES OF SHAWTY LO

Shawty Lo

Carlos Rico Walker always considered himself the "King of Bankhead." Located on the Westside of Atlanta, Bankhead Highway (now Donald Lee Hollowell Parkway), was known as a thoroughfare where black culture existed while amid extreme poverty and crime. When Walker was a child, more than forty-five percent of the residents in the Bankhead area lived below the poverty level; a rate that doubled the average for the city of Atlanta. But the setbacks never deterred the people in the community. The area sparked the first ideas of prominent Atlanta rappers such as André 3000, T.I., Kilo Ali, Young Dro, and Diamond D, all who lived on or near Bankhead during their youth. Diamond D, along with D-Roc of the Ying Yang Twins, would put Bankhead on the map nationally with the Bankhead Bounce dance during the mid-1990s. Michael Jackson even paid homage to the dance during a performance at the 1995 MTV Music Awards.

Two public housing projects existed on Bankhead until 2011, Bankhead Courts and Bowen Homes. Walker, known in the neighborhood as Shawty Lo, was raised in Bowen Homes.

Built-in 1966, Bowen Homes paid homage to John

Wesley Edward Bowen, a former slave who became one of the first blacks in America to receive a Ph.D when he earned it from Boston College in 1887. Bowen would later move to Atlanta where he served as a prominent clergyman until he died in 1933.

When it initially opened, Bowen Homes was viewed as a city within a city as it became the largest housing project in Atlanta and featured an elementary school, library, and a daycare center.

The Gate City Day Care Center would make national headlines in 1980 during the height of the Atlanta Child Murders. At 4-years-old, Shawty Lo was one of eighty-three kids who attended the Gate City Day Care Center on the morning of October 13, 1980. Shortly after 10:00 a.m., a massive explosion occurred at the daycare center. The ceiling collapsed, and bricks from a wall were blown into the air as white smoke filled the entire center. One child ran out of the building with his arm detached from his body, and others fled the building while bleeding and with severe burn wounds. Five kids and two adults were found dead following the explosion.

Initial reactions from residents in the Bowen Homes community was that the explosion was set by the individuals or individual responsible for the Atlanta Child Murders. Authorities would quiet those theories by saying that the blast occurred due to gas leaking from a faulty furnace inside of the daycare center.

That day, Shawty Lo followed his instincts. Once the explosion occurred, teachers instructed the kids to line up behind each other to leave the building in an orderly fashion. Shawty Lo ran from the building without hesitation. He would later reveal that some of those kids who remained in line did not make it out.

Shawty Lo would learn to play by his own rules at an early age. Sometimes the consequences were beneficial, and other times the results were detrimental. In a sense, it was the only way that he knew how to survive for nothing ever came easy to Shawty Lo.

"My momma was on drugs, so I was raised by my grandmother," Shawty Lo said during an interview in 2011. "My grandmother died from cancer when I was 17. People thought that I would be dead before 17. I got arrested twenty-eight times, and I've been convicted four times. I was once facing twenty-to-forty years [in prison]. But I only served one year. When I got out, I came back to the music."

Known as a prominent drug dealer on Atlanta's Westside in the 1990s, Shawty Lo decided to leave the street life behind and try his hand at a new game. By the mid-2000s, music became a prosperous industry in Atlanta as young men and women could go from poverty and lower middle-class to earning six or seven-figure salaries in a matter of months. Shawty Lo knew that if he could turn his street hustle into a rap hustle, he would be next in line to experience success in music. His first step to stardom began on his block.

Shawty Lo took money that he saved from hustling and opened a makeshift studio and founded the independent record label, D4L (Down 4 Life). He enlisted a crew of rappers and producers from his neighborhood to work on a project that would serve as the first release on the record label.

Rappers Fabo, Mook B, and Stuntman would join Shawty Lo to form the group which held the same name as the label, D4L. K-Rab (Krazy Rythm and Beats), a producer from Atlanta's Westside, would craft a new sound that would change the music scene. The first audience to hear the unique sound was clubgoers who partied at a small nightclub on Bankhead Highway known as the Poole Palace.

Shawty Lo and his crew would frequent the Poole Palace on Thursday nights and weekends during the early 2000s. They were often joined by hundreds of clubgoers who would cram inside of the humid venue, which had the feel of a basement house party. The Poole Palace distinguished itself from most clubs in Midtown and Buckhead because it allowed new artists and producers to test their music. K-Rab, along with Born Immaculate and Broderick Thompson Smith, created the snap music sound by producing songs such as "Bubble Gum" and "Do It, Do It (Poole Palace)." But it was K-Rab's collaboration with Shawty Lo and his group D4L (Down 4 Life) that set the snap music subgenre in motion.

In October of 2005, D4L released the snap music song "Laffy Taffy," which served as an alternative to the elbow-throwing aggression of crunk music. When DJs played the song "Laffy Taffy," clubgoers would snap their fingers while bouncing from right to left, giving a slightly new spin to the two-step. The hook, rapped by the hyperactive Fabo, proved to be catchy, fun, and served as an easy transition to pop radio.

Three months after its initial release, "Laffy Taffy" earned the No. 1 spot on the Billboard charts, dethroning Mariah Carey and her hit, "Don't Forget About Us." D4L's "Laffy Taffy" would break the Guinness World Record for being the most downloaded song in the history of music in 2007 and went on to sell three times platinum. The group would follow "Laffy Taffy" with another snap music hit, "Betcha Can't Do It Like Me." Snap music, the subgenre of rap created in the Bankhead community, found its way into mainstream pop culture.

D4L's national exposure opened the doors for other snap music groups such as Dem Franchize Boyz. The four-man group released the snap music hit "White Tee" before signing with Jermaine Dupri's So So Def records. The group followed "White Tee" with the hit songs "I Think They Like Me" and "Lean Wit It, Rock Wit It."

At a time when snap music stood as the Atlanta sound that garnered most of the national attention, Shawty Lo would distance himself from the subgenre by making music that focused on his hustling days in the Bowen Homes projects. Shawty Lo spit rhymes in a low-pitched tone as if he were telling ghost stories from the Trap. On the song, "I'm Da Man," produced by K-Rab, Shawty Lo described his matrimony to the drug game which included a life of money, fast cars, and faster consequences.

In 2008, Shawty Lo would get the opportunity to give his full perspective of life in Bowen Homes with his debut album, *Units in the City*. The album's lead single, "Dey Know," was driven by trumpets sampled from the song "Children of the Sun" by the funk-jazz band, Mandrill. In the video, Shawty Lo took viewers to the heart of Bowen Homes and Bankhead while paying homage to marching bands from the South. The song's star-studded remix, known as the "Dirty South" remix, featured verses from Jeezy, Ludacris, Plies, and Lil Wayne.

On the follow-up single, "Dunn, Dunn," Shawty Lo would take aim at T.I. by questioning his affiliation with the Bankhead neighborhood. The beef between the two began after T.I. allegedly rejected an offer to rap on a song with Shawty Lo. He also claimed that T.I. dissed him with a lyric on the song, "Big S--t Poppin." They would engage in a battle of words as T.I. would respond to Shawty Lo's, "Dunn Dunn" with the song "What's Up, What's Happening." In the video, T.I. taunted Shawty Lo by rapping in a lawn chair while sitting at the entrance of Bowen Homes.

The two would eventually squash their beef following a brief scuffle between their respective entourages during the 2008 Dirty Awards which took place at the Georgia International Center in Atlanta. In March of 2009, Shawty Lo and T.I. would appear together on stage at Club Crucial to declare an end to their rap beef.

In the years following the release of *Units in the City*, Shawty Lo's life outside of music would garner the most attention. He faced health issues due to complications from diabetes and was hospitalized in December of 2011. Shawty Lo would use his platform to share the importance of diabetes awareness by serving as a spokesperson for the American Diabetes Association.

But he also gained negative press after he attempted to show the dynamics of his family with the 2013 reality TV show, "All My Babies' Mommas." Bought by Oxygen Media, the reality TV show would feature Shawty Lo and the ten mothers of his eleven children. A petition from Change.org claimed the show "exploits and stereotypes Black children and families." Within one week after the release of the first promotional video of "All My Babies' Mommas," Oxygen Media canceled the show.

With his plan for a reality TV show crushed, Shawty

Lo focused on his sophomore album after signing a distribution deal with 50 Cent's G-Unit South. However, Shawty Lo never got an opportunity to release his second album.

On September 21, 2016, Shawty Lo died in a one-car accident while driving on I-285 near Cascade Road in Atlanta. He was 40-years old.

I attended Shawty Lo's funeral on October 10, 2016. Held at the Jackson Memorial Baptist Church on Atlanta's Westside, nearly three thousand family members, friends, and fans attended the homegoing service. Shawty Lo's kids brought many of the attendees to tears by sharing stories of their father and revealing how he made it a point to give back to families who struggled financially in the Bankhead community.

Seven days after he was laid to rest, Shawty Lo would receive the ultimate tribute by the most powerful entertainer of this generation. Before a capacity crowd of seventy thousand-plus at the Georgia Dome in Atlanta, Beyoncé took a moment to pay tribute to Shawty Lo. While singing her hit "Diva," Beyoncé danced to Shawty Lo's "Dey Know." The entire Georgia Dome erupted. But it was more than a tribute to Shawty Lo. It was music's most significant star taking a moment to recognize an artist whose life was initially saved by music.

Shawty Lo never claimed to be the most prominent artist in rap because it was more important for him to be the most significant rapper from Bankhead. He knew that if he could make it out of Bankhead, it would serve as a glimmer of hope for those who felt trapped.

Beyoncé and Shawty Lo represented two completely different aspects of black music. As she danced to Shawty Lo's "Dey Know," there was a brief connection that existed between the two. If Shawty Lo could inspire music's most renowned artist, there's another kid from Bankhead who can do the same and possibly even more. "My thing was to always put Bankhead and Bowen Homes on the map," Shawty Lo said in 2011.

In the years to come, crunk and snap music would subside as Trap music added a new narrative to the story of Atlanta.

CHAPTER V

TRAP BECOMES MUSIC: THE JOURNEY OF T.I.

T.I.

Turmoil followed T.I. throughout the early stages of his career, but his life before music was even more turbulent. Born as Clifford Harris on September 25, 1980, T.I.'s youth consisted of being raised in the Center Hill neighborhood off of Bankhead Highway, an area on the Westside of Atlanta with a history of slum housing and poor living conditions.

In 1970, a decade before T.I.'s birth, Bankhead Courts became the second public housing project to open on Bankhead Highway following the construction of Bowen Homes in 1966. The Atlanta Housing Authority decided to build Bankhead Courts on a site used for dumping waste. As a result, over seventeen hundred residents who lived in the five hundred unit housing complex endured sewage and plumbing problems for decades. By 1989, the violence in Bankhead Courts became so severe that the U.S. Postal Service would not deliver mail to residents. Southern Bell, the city's phone company at the time, limited telephone repairs and installations to one day per week. And MARTA suspended bus service in the area after a bus driver allegedly saw a man holding a gun in the bushes.

The residents of the entire Bankhead community felt neglected without much hope of finding a way out.

By the age of 17, T.I. found himself in a place where an escape from the Bankhead area seemed impossible. He was arrested on numerous occasions and convicted in Cobb County, Georgia in 1998 for possession of crack cocaine with intent to distribute. While most of his peers at Fredrick Douglass High School were preparing for graduation, T.I. was on the verge of becoming another victim of the Trap. That was until he found a way to channel his inner conflict and turn it into music.

Nicknamed Tip as a youth, T.I. initially began rapping under the name T.I.P. His skills as a rapper became evident to two of his acquaintances, Aldrin "DJ Toomp" Davis and Jason Geter, who were both involved in the music industry in some form. As mentioned earlier, Toomp served as the DJ for one of Atlanta's first rappers, MC Shy D.

A few years later, Toomp moved to Miami and worked with Luther Campbell and the 2 Live Crew. Toomp produced 2 Live Crew's "In the Dust," a song that alludes to the U.S. government's role in distributing drugs to poor black communities. It was an accusation that was found to be true with the uncovering of the Iran-Contra scandal starting in 1982. Under the direction of Oliver North and the Ronald Reagan presidential administration, the CIA used the money earned from drug sales in inner-city Los Angeles to fund the Contra revolution in Nicaragua. "In the Dust" appeared on the soundtrack to *New Jack City*, a film released in 1991 about New York's rising crack cocaine epidemic. It was a rare Southern rap track that garnered national exposure during the early 1990s. However, Toomp never received credit for his production.

Jason Geter, a native of New York who relocated to Atlanta, worked at Patchwerk Studios in West Midtown, Atlanta, a staple in the city's music industry as it served as the recording home for artists such as TLC, OutKast, Jermaine Dupri, and others. In the spring of 1999, Jeter, who would become T.I.P's first manager, set up a meeting with Kawan "KP" Prather who was in a session at Patchwerk Studios. Prather made a name for himself in the music industry first as an artist in the group Parental Advisory and as the vice president of A&R at LaFace Records. He was instrumental in the careers of artists such as OutKast, Goodie Mob, and YoungBloodz. Following his success as an A&R, Prather started an imprint, Ghet-O-Vision, which had distribution through LaFace/Arista Records. Searching for new talent to join the label, Prather knew that he struck gold from the moment he witnessed a teenaged T.I.P. rapping over an instrumental on that fateful day at Patchwerk Studios.

T.I.P. went from serving in an Atlanta Trap to flying nearly two thousand miles away after KP took him on a trip to the 1999 Source Awards in Los Angeles. T.I.P. eventually signed to Ghet-O-Vision/LaFace Records. Due to Q-Tip of A Tribe Called Quest being signed to Arista at the same time, the label suggested T.I.P. shorten his name to T.I. to eliminate potential confusion in terms of marketing the two artists. But there was no doubt that T.I. would stand alone in rap with his delivery, style, and sound.

"When I first met T.I., I noticed that he was a smart and attentive dude," Kawan "KP" Prather told me during an interview. "With him being from Bankhead, we got along because I grew up in every part of Atlanta. Born in Vine City, moved to College Park, then Oakland City, and then back to College Park. So it was like meeting a best friend that I had known already. He was instantly my little brother because he wanted to be great. He was talented but 'coachable.' We were in a studio session with [rap group] P.A. that day. The first thing I asked him was, 'So you rap? Why don't you rap on this record?' With no hesitation, no fear, he just walked in the booth and roasted the track."

To help mold his sound, T.I. decided to record with DJ Toomp as his primary producer. After his stint with Luther Campbell and 2 Live Crew in Miami, Toomp eventually returned to Atlanta where he produced for local artists, held down gigs as a DJ, and cut hair on the side to make ends meet. Nearly a decade would pass before Toomp would get the opportunity to produce a breakout hit following "In the Dust."

Toomp's home in the Ben Hill neighborhood of Atlanta served as a studio, makeshift barbershop, and hangout spot. T.I. would often visit Toomp for hours and occasionally get a haircut or write to a beat that Toomp had produced.

One afternoon, Toomp found himself putting the finishing touches on a newly produced track when T.I. and a few of his friends arrived. Within seconds of hearing Toomp's instrumental, T.I. approached Toomp and said, "That's mine!"

When producing the track, Toomp found inspiration from production by UGK's Pimp C, who had a knack for incorporating church organs and blues guitars in his production, giving his music a soulful, down-home feel. A lot of UGK's early production was reminiscent of music created by bands such as The Meters and Booker T. & the M.G.'s.

Toomp used an ASR-10 and MPC62 beat machine to produce the track. His only desire was to make what Pimp C would call a "Country rap tune."

"I was in UGK mode," Toomp recalled about producing the track. "It was all Texas with the church organs. Pimp C was the king of the ASR. I watched Pimp C cook up a few of those tracks right on the spot. With my track, I was able to incorporate a real clean organ, and I just started to bang it out. But we weren't thinking Trap [music] at all. Basically just making country rap songs. After T.I. ended up putting the concept to it, everyone fell in love with it. Like, 'Yo, that's got to go on that album.'"

T.I. wrote to Toomp's beat and provided an unfiltered look inside an open drug market in Atlanta. He called the song, "Dope Boyz [In the Trap]." T.I. took the position of a street-level drug dealer by describing how quantities of drugs are broken down and sold. He also called out sections of Atlanta where a high concentration of drug activity took place at the time, making it a point to identify those locations as the Trap.

"It was really about being a voice for the voiceless," T.I. told me during an interview in Atlanta in 2017. "It was about representing people that I felt weren't hearing their lives narrated through music. At the time, it was crunk, conscious, and booty-shaking music [in Atlanta]. You were either crunk like Lil John or you was conscious like OutKast, Goodie Mob, and Dungeon

Family. No one was telling dope boy stories. OutKast would touch on it and so would Goodie Mob, but overall they were very conscious and aware. So my purpose with 'Dope Boyz' was really to make a song for us. I wanted to make a song that talks about us and how we live our lives and the shit that we go through. That's what I set out to do."

Featured on T.I.'s debut album *I'm Serious*, "Dope Boyz [In the Trap]" proved to be the signature song on a critically-acclaimed album that never reached its full commercial potential. When it came down to record sales, T.I.'s debut could not compete with the outstanding numbers achieved by his LaFace labelmates OutKast, TLC, and Usher. *I'm Serious* lacked prominent record sales, but painted a raw picture of Atlanta's street culture.

"We would go from city-to-city, and the crowds would go crazy when they heard 'Dope Boyz,'" Toomp recalled. "Even the dope boys in each city would come to the shows, and they were feeling that song. They would be in VIP buying bottles, but they all wanted to holler at T.I. They were true fans, and they liked that we were talking their talk."

In one last effort to give *I'm Serious* a much-needed push, T.I. decided to use his own money to fund a video for "Dope Boyz." The low-budget video lacked quality from a production standpoint, but it helped to give credence to the song. Years before cellphone footage became common, the "Dope Boyz" video's dark and grainy footage provided a realistic look at the grittiness that existed in the Trap.

Before releasing the video to the public, T.I., Jason

Geter, and DJ Toomp took a trip to New York to give Arista Records president L.A. Reid a preview of the video.

"After seeing the success of 'Dope Boyz,' we did an independent video and we played it for L.A. Reid," Toomp shared with me. "But he snuck out of the building on us. We were like, 'Yo, is L.A. coming back?' We sat in there for about an hour. We thought he was just taking a [restroom] break or something. That man left the building. He left me, Jason Geter, and T.I. We played the video and I guess he was like, 'Man, I done had enough' [Toomp laughed]."

L.A. Reid may not have understood how music inspired by the Trap could correlate into major record sales, at the time. As a result, T.I. would eventually be dropped from LaFace Records.

"I have to be honest, I don't know much about Trap," L.A. Reid told me years later when I asked him about signing T.I. to LaFace Records and, a decade later, signing Future to Epic Records.

"I just know the artists who I desire to work with. Whether it's OutKast, T.I., or Future. It's something in the water in Atlanta. It's something in that Georgia red clay that's special. But if you know me, I don't put music in a box. I can't give it a name. But I don't know what Trap is [Reid laughed]. All I know is if it has a melody or if it doesn't."

BACK TO THE TRAP

The moment T.I. parted ways with LaFace Records, the rapper had thoughts of returning to the Trap. But

T.I. took another chance at music by betting on himself. Independent at the time, T.I. went back into the studio with DJ Toomp, his rap crew P$C (Pimp Squad Click), and DJ Drama to release the *In da Streets* mixtape series. The buzz surrounding his mixtapes created a bidding war between top major record labels. Atlantic Records presented the most lucrative offer and T.I. reportedly signed a 10-year multi-million dollar record deal.

With his first album on Atlantic Records, T.I. continued to build on the theme introduced on the song "Dope Boyz." But instead of highlighting it on just one song, T.I. would take listeners on a 67-minute journey through the Trap.

"The purpose of *I'm Serious* was that I wanted to show that people down South can really rap," T.I. shared with me. "I wanted people to know that we can really kick verses. I didn't want anybody to put me in a box because I was from [Atlanta]. But now the flip side of that became a curse of that gift. When my album dropped, nobody could recognize where I was from because it was all over the place. So for the next album, I decided that there weren't going to be any questions. We decided to do the whole album on straight Trap shit. So that next album, *Trap Muzik*, it was very in your face, raw, unapologetic, and it was hard to misconstrue anything else."

On August 19, 2003, Grand Hustle Records with distribution by Atlantic Records released *Trap Muzik* to the public. The album presented itself as a coming-of-age story from the perspective of a wayward teen who viewed selling drugs as his best chance out of poverty. From the onset, T.I. allowed listeners to delve into the mindset of those who occupy the Trap. It opened with the unapologetic DJ Toomp-produced track, "Trap Muzik."

"When we did 'Dope Boyz' that was not considered a 'Trap' song," DJ Toomp explained. "We didn't use 'Trap' as the title for the music that we were doing. But once that song broke through, we decided to make an album that focused on the whole lifestyle of Trapping. So it wasn't just about the sound of the music; it was more about the content."

The album begins with the attitude of getting money at all costs even if that means standing on the corner for hours, selling in the cold and rain, or using violence to intimidate the competition. *Trap Muzik* has moments of braggadocio, materialism, misogyny, and violence. But T.I. also shows the internal guilt of dealing drugs in his community.

While rapping over a Kanye West-produced track that sampled Bloodstones' song "I'm Just Doing My Job," T.I. provided an open letter to the residents of the Trap as the song reveals itself as a dope boy's mea culpa. The Trap was never a place where street-level drug dealers desired to be, but it was the only place that would have them.

The David Banner-produced hit single "Rubberband Man" and "Let's Get Away," produced by Jazze Pha, proved that T.I. could make songs that garner radio spins while maintaining a street edge.

On "Be Better Than Me," T.I. stripped away the glamour of the Trap. He raps about the mandatory minimum sentences that once led to 25 years-to-life in prison for possession of more than four ounces of crack cocaine. The underlying message of the song was that school or college has a bigger payoff than the Trap.

"I grew up in Bankhead, been around Campbellton Road, Simpson Road, West End, and every ghetto in Atlanta," T.I. shared with me during an interview in 2013. "I never thought it was cooler to go to jail than to go to college. If you would've given me the option between jail and college, I'm taking college. On the other hand, we knew that we were doing things that could land us in jail. But we never thought it was cool, that's a misconception. If you're a teenager, don't believe that going to jail is cool. I've been in there with people who are doing 20-year bids and life sentences. Those folks never feel like it's cool."

Overall, *Trap Muzik* is a project that provides street ethos and an introspective look at the Trap.

"With *Trap Muzik*, T.I. and DJ Toomp created a soundtrack to a Southern urban environment," Killer Mike shared. "Every music starts in a real anonymous place. The first time someone sang about love, it was probably real and earnest. At some point, they figured out that this was how you get girls to listen to the record. With *Trap Muzik*, T.I. and Toomp dropped a very realistic view of what was happening in the Bluff, what was happening in Bankhead, and what was happening in Adamsville. They gave you a perspective, and the sound was so dope that other people took the sound and built upon it. So you have Trap music which interprets what it's like to be in a Trap."

I sat in a federal courtroom as a reporter in the fall of 2007 as T.I. faced illegal weapons charges. Two weeks prior, following the rehearsal at the BET Hip Hop

Awards, T.I. allegedly met with a person who delivered him three machine guns and two silencers. The person who set up the transaction was a bodyguard-turned-informant. T.I. was arrested at the scene. When police raided his home, they found several more loaded guns. As a convicted felon, T.I. was prohibited from owning a firearm

The man who helped to put Trap music on the map was suddenly facing the possibility of being trapped behind bars for up to twenty years of his life.

T.I. pleaded guilty to unlawfully possessing machine guns and silencers and possession of firearms by a convicted felon. He would serve one year and a day in federal prison.

T.I. found a way to escape the societal barriers of Bankhead, drug convictions, and that 2007 federal gun case. The drugs, guns, and bad decisions made early in his career were only pieces of a man who would later become a philanthropist, giving father, and activist. He was able to fight another day and tell the story of the Trap and the people who never made it out.

When T.I. and executive producers DJ Toomp and Jason Geter began working on *Trap Muzik*, the primary objective was to prove the talent and worth of an Atlanta-based rapper.

"At the end of the day, the whole Trap movement started from the *Trap Muzik* album," Jason Geter shared. "We were taking it to the forefront of the world. It's interesting and impressive. It makes you feel good just knowing how you have a product that has inspired the world in more ways than one. A lot of people don't even know where Trap came from. But one of the first records to use the term Trap is T.I's album, *Trap Muzik*, in 2003."

Trap Muzik would eventually set the foundation for a new sound and era in hip-hop.

Trap History

CHAPTER VI

THE RISE OF TRAP MUSIC: JEEZY, THE BMF TAKEOVER, AND THE ERA OF MIXTAPES

Jeezy

In one night, I witnessed hip-hop, Atlanta's street scene, and the entire music industry enter a new day. It was early January of 2005 when a few friends and I decided to go out for the evening. At some point that night, we found ourselves at Vision Nightclub.

Vision Nightclub was a sleek nightspot located in Midtown, Atlanta on Peachtree Street. Most clubgoers were upwardly mobile young adults and college students who maintained a love for Trap music. In the early 2000s, Vision Nightclub, owned by Alex and Michael Gideon, stood as a high-profile urban nightclub in the Atlanta area. It became Atlanta's version of New York's famous Studio 54 that reigned during the disco music era of the 1970s. On any given night, it was common to see top music acts such as Jay-Z, Russell Simmons, Diddy, and Britney Spears partying with stars of the Atlanta music industry. If you were somebody or wanted to be somebody in Atlanta's growing entertainment industry, you found a way to get inside of Vision Nightclub.

Most of the events at Vision were star-studded, but one night stood out as a moment that had the feel of a movie premiere. Far from Hollywood, this event put a spotlight on the Trap stars.

Shortly before midnight, traffic remained at a standstill on Peachtree Street as a motorcade of Bentleys, Lamborghinis, and black Cadillac Escalades were all in tow. A massive line outside of Vision stretched down the street and was occupied by women with modelesque figures who wore skintight dresses, heels, and held high-end clutch purses. Most of the men in line wore suits and blazers as if they were headed to a corporate function—staying true to the dress code that prohibited sneakers, jeans, or athletic wear. Inside of the spacious three-level venue, clubgoers were shoulder-to-shoulder as moving an inch in any direction became a task. Security would make room for a line of bottle service girls who sashayed through the crowd while holding bottles of expensive champagne above their heads. Sparklers that were attached to the top of each bottle signaled their entrance into the VIP where some paid up to one thousand dollars to sit in an exclusive section. The night was all in anticipation for the release of a mixtape.

Before that night, albums were still the gold standard and mixtapes were primarily used as a way for unsigned artists to get their music to DJs who worked on radio and at nightclubs. But the release of Young Jeezy's *Trap or Die* changed how consumers and the industry viewed mixtapes.

"Atlanta was just a different place, period," Jeezy shared with me a decade after the release. "It was more festive, there were more things going on, and definitely a lot more money flowing. That was a good time for us when it came to music and the streets. It was for all the people who you were still out here on their grind and pushing to do better. It was for the streets, for the people, and for the culture."

Born Jay Jenkins, Young Jeezy, who would later drop 'Young' from his rap name, was a street-savvy rapper from Hawkinsville, Georgia which is about ninety minutes south of Atlanta. Early in his career, Jeezy had ambitions of being the next Master P by turning his street hustle into owning a legit record company. He established Corporate Thugz Entertainment in 2001 and released an independent album, *Thuggin' Under the Influence*, under the name Lil J. Two years later, he released *Come Shop wit Me*, which featured Atlanta rappers Lil Jon, Pastor Troy, and Bone Crusher.

Jeezy's independent releases sold a respectable amount of units, but his career took off after he connected with DJ Drama for the Gangsta Grillz mixtape series. The summer before the release of the *Trap or Die* mixtape, Jeezy and DJ Drama met to work on a previous mixtape entitled, Tha *Streets Iz Watchin*.

"The first time I met Jeezy was with [his manager] Coach K," DJ Drama shared, referring to the industry veteran who once managed Jeezy, Gucci Mane, and formed Quality Control Music with Pierre Thomas in 2012. "We went to Harry & Sons restaurant for lunch. I had just done my first Gangsta Grillz party at Club Fuel in Buckhead. Jeezy told me he was there and he was watching from afar. He told me his whole vision for *Tha Streets Iz Watchin*. It came out in the summer of 2004, and it caught on. That was the first Gangsta Grillz mixtape that I ever got paid for."

Tha *Streets Iz Watchin* featured the standout tracks "Over Here" and "Air Forces." It was a perfect precursor to the release of *Trap or Die*.

"Mixtapes were not a Southern thing," Nick Love, former marketing director at Corporate Thugz Entertainment, told me during a 2018 interview. "50 Cent had done the mixtape thing and that started as a New York movement. When *Trap or Die* comes, it changed everything. I remember Jeezy said we would press up one million copies of the mixtape. The cases would come in a box and CDs and inserts would come in separate boxes. We [the CTE team] put all of those mixtapes together by hand in our office on Bishop Street. I asked, 'when are we going to ship these to retail?' We had a meeting and Jeezy said that we would be giving each CD away for free. The first run was fifty thousand. It took us weeks to put all of those CDs together."

When the mixtape finally dropped, it created a seismic shift in the music industry and ignited Jeezy's career. It led to two record deals as Jeezy signed on as a solo act for Def Jam and signed to Bad Boy Records as a member of the group, Boyz N Da Hood.

A MAFIA'S TALE

On the night of the *Trap or Die* mixtape release party, two crews surrounded Young Jeezy. Corporate Thugz Entertainment, which mostly consisted of rappers and producers who were signed or affiliated with Jeezy's independent label. The other crew that flanked Jeezy that night was known as BMF.

The Black Mafia Family would often arrive at events in Atlanta with dozens of crew members in tow. They were the guys who drove the Bentleys, Porsches, and Ferraris. They were the ones who spent thousands of dollars in one night on bottle service. They were the guys who could excite the aspiring models who would break a high heel just for a chance to sit next to them in a crowded VIP area of the club. And even a few male groupies who wanted to make it appear as if they were down with the most notorious crew in the city. The streets of Atlanta belonged to BMF, and they wanted every person in their vicinity to know.

BMF had the prestige of platinum-selling rap artists, but the music never served as their primary source of income. Headed by brothers Demetrius "Big Meech" Flenory and Terry "Southwest T" Flenory, BMF became known as the most prominent drug crew to infiltrate Atlanta since the Miami Boys. At the height of their reign, it's estimated that the Flenory brothers were worth more than $270 million.

Raised by both parents in a strict religious household, the Flenory brothers were expected to attend church regularly. Prayer and Bible study were a necessity. They kept their faith as a family, but it was hard to ignore severe financial issues.

The Flenorys were one of many families stricken by poverty in Detroit, Michigan. In the early 1990s, Detroit's black unemployment rate was at an alarming forty percent as surrounding industries began massive layoffs and closures. The fall of a once-thriving American city became evident during that decade.

During their youth, Terry and Demetrius' school wardrobe consisted of off-brand sneakers and a few shirts and jeans they would share every other day. By the time they reached puberty, Demetrius and Terry were looking for a way to escape from their family's economic struggles.

Several crime organizations controlled the streets of Detroit during the 1980s and '90s. Drug dealing crews such as Young Boys Incorporated; the Chamber Brothers; Best Friends Gang; and Maserati Rick made millions and left a bloody trail in the Motor City. As teens, the Flenory brothers witnessed how street hustlers were making money from the drug trade and began selling $50 bags of crack cocaine on street corners.

But their days of selling drugs on a street corner ended once they began working with a person who, reportedly, had ties to a Mexican cartel and could supply a vast amount of pure and uncut cocaine. In a matter of years, the Flenory brothers were not just street-level dealers anymore; they became the suppliers. The brothers developed a distribution network that supplied cities across the nation, with Terry operating in Los Angeles and Big Meech setting up shop in Atlanta. The brothers also had hubs in St. Louis and Detroit.

Big Meech's arrival in Atlanta coincided with the city's burgeoning music scene. Witnessing the prosperity within urban music, Big Meech began to explore ways to delve into entertainment with the creation of a record label, BMF Entertainment, and a magazine, *The Juice*.

BMF signed an artist by the name of Bleu DaVinci, hosted lavish parties at nightclubs around the city to promote the company, and purchased billboards that stood on I-75 North and Peachtree Road highlighting the BMF brand. If there was an attempt to go legit, it came at a time when BMF was still assumed by many to be drug traffickers.

"When *Trap or Die* came out, the BMF billboard was

up, and it said, 'The World is BMF's,'" Nick Love recalled. "The first time I saw it, I thought it was audacious and brazen. I remember going to Lenox Mall with my girl and shopping on an off day. I saw Lamborghini cars, BMWs, and [Mercedes] Benzes pull up back-to-back into the mall's valet. There were about sixteen or seventeen cars. They [BMF] decided to go to the top floor at Lenox Mall and shoot an impromptu music video. I know Atlanta like the back of my hand. Atlanta as a city had never seen that type of movement and money from young black males. And we all knew where they were getting their money from."

During the FBI's investigation of BMF years later, the authorities noted that the organization owned a fleet of vehicles equipped with secret deoxygenated compartments used for smuggling drugs and weapons. The Drug Enforcement Agency confiscated a Hummer H2 limousine during a raid on a property owned by BMF members in 2004. Three years later and after selling the Hummer to a private citizen at an auction, the FBI searched for the Hummer with the hopes of finding more evidence. Once they found the vehicle, they tore it apart rummaging for secret compartments. During their search, agents allegedly discovered seven hidden semiautomatic firearms and $900,000 in cash believed to be the property of BMF members.

The FBI eventually built a case against BMF based on wiretaps on Terry Flenory's phone calls. The wiretaps led to indictments of Terry, Big Meech, and one hundred and fifty defendants in six states. One of the codefendants, Tremayne Graham, was married to the daughter of Shirley Franklin, who served as mayor of

Atlanta during the height of BMF's reign. Franklin's daughter, Kai Franklin Graham, pleaded guilty to money laundering but only received probation for her involvement. The Flenory brothers were handed 30-year prison sentences for cocaine distribution and money laundering.

The incarceration of top BMF members marked an end to many of the prominent black drug organizations that once ruled Atlanta. Instead, independent dealers were usually supplied with drugs by Mexican cartels. The rising price of a kilo of cocaine also made it more difficult for new crews to duplicate the reign of BMF and the Miami Boys.

"Dope is so high now, the average dealer can't afford it at $40,000 per kilo [of cocaine]," DJ Toomp told me in 2015. "But back then [the 1980s and '90s], it was between 17K and maybe 22K. Now guys are finessing. Finessing comes from the fact that dope is so high that these guys have fake birds [kilos]. You think you're getting more. But when you cook it, you find out that it has a whole lot of baby formula or something other than what you paid for."

MY PRESIDENT IS BLACK

In the summer of 2008, Jeezy arguably released the most important rap song of that year. The entire concept came about in June after Jeezy received an instrumental from producer The Bizness. Instantly inspired by the beat, Jeezy decided to write.

On the same day, Barack Obama defeated Hilary Clinton to become the Democratic presidential nominee. It was also the first time a black candidate led a major party ticket. Although Obama accomplished a major achievement by becoming the Democratic nominee, he still faced an uphill battle. Along with the obvious obstacle of being a black man, some viewed Obama as too young and inexperienced to lead the country.

But Jeezy decided to make a bold prediction. On June 3, 2008, Jeezy completed the first version of "My President Is Black." The song detailed Jeezy's thoughts on poverty, mass incarceration, and other issues faced by a multitude of blacks in America. But it also featured a chorus that became a rallying cry for change and speaks to achieving the impossible.

When Def Jam officially released the single as "My President" in August 2008, Nas added a verse, and the video was directed by Gabriel Hart on Auburn Avenue in Atlanta in front of the historic Ebenezer Baptist Church. Jay-Z would add another verse to the song months later. Once Barack Obama made history on November 4, 2008, by becoming the 44th President of the United States, "My President" became the official song that summed up the thoughts and dreams of an entire generation. Hundreds of rap songs were released in 2008, but "My President" stood alone as a significant work of art that defined an era.

Oddly enough, Jeezy shared a story with me on how he was dissed by President Obama years after releasing "My President." The way Jeezy explained it, President Obama invited him to a private dinner in New York. But when Jeezy arrived at the address given, he had issues gaining clearance inside.

"[President Obama] had me come to a dinner and

they wouldn't let me inside," Jeezy shared. "I was invited to a dinner he had in New York. When I got to the door, the Secret Service told my team that I couldn't come inside because there was some type of security issue. They probably Googled me. I felt a certain way because I felt as if I did a lot to help his campaign. I believed in his cause. I initially felt unappreciated."

But President Obama would later give a subtle salute to Jeezy that gave the president more credibility in the rap community while confusing most middle-aged politicians. During the White House Correspondents' Dinner in Washington, D.C. on April 28, 2012, President Obama told the audience, "In my first term, I sang Al Green, in my second term, I'm going with Young Jeezy." President Obama later joked that he sings Jeezy's songs to first lady Michelle Obama at times.

"He later came back and shouted me out," Jeezy said referring to President Obama's joke at the White House Correspondents' Dinner. "That let me know what type of person he is as a man. There are so many ways that he could've done that. But he did it on his platform and on his time. It was like being an artist and me shouting out my homie. It feels great."

For Jeezy, President Obama's small gesture proved that he was a stand-up guy and man of his word.

"He was in a room full of politicians and major people like Oprah," Jeezy said. "I'm sure a lot of people wondered how he knew about me. It was his way of saying, 'Look, I understand everything that you're doing, but you have a criminal past, you can't stand next to me right now.' But he decided to acknowledge me from afar. To me, that was presidential. He knows that we have a pulse on the culture. It was great to be appreciated by him."

THE POWER OF MIXTAPES

The change within Atlanta's drug scene coincided with a significant change in the music industry. Some law enforcement treated music distribution as if it were illegal drugs. The success of mixtapes threatened the Recording Industry Association of America. To the RIAA, mixtapes were pirated material. Two years following the release of *Trap or Die*, the FBI and RIAA would make a bold move to criminalize the creators of music.

On an afternoon in January of 2007, dozens of FBI agents and police kicked down the doors of an office owned by DJ Drama and his business partners, Aphilliates Music Group. Officers forced DJ Drama and DJ Cannon to the floor and placed handcuffs on their wrists. During the arrest, officers confiscated 81,000 mixtape CDs, computers, recording equipment, and four cars. All of the assets owned by DJ Drama, DJ Cannon, and DJ Sense were frozen as they were held on $100,000 bond.

DJ Drama, a graduate of Clark Atlanta University, never sold dope. However, he was facing the same felony charges that put drug dealers and high-level criminal organizations away for years. DJ Drama was arrested under the Racketeer Influenced and Corrupt Organization Act (known as RICO). The RICO Act led to the conviction of members of the Miami Boys and BMF. But instead of cocaine, DJ Drama was handed those charges because he distributed mixtapes.

"I just think the music game was at a point where it was changing in so many ways and record sales were low," DJ Drama said. "I think it was just a breakdown in communication when it came to what we were doing on a street level and how it was helping record companies. The marketing department understood, but the legal department didn't get it. There was some fear. But through that arrest, it opened up a lot of doors. The entire industry learned from it. The RIAA learned from it, my team learned from it, and artists learned from it. Now the mixtapes business is larger than ever."

Mixtapes eventually became essential to the marketing and success of hip-hop artists. Independent mixtapes allowed artists to experiment musically and build a fan base before releasing an official project. Jeezy's *Trap or Die* was one of the first mixtapes to establish this model.

Young Jeezy's initial rise in music, often linked to BMF's backstory, offered another side of the Trap. Artists and producers soon began to follow the standard presented by T.I., Young Jeezy, and their primary producers DJ Toomp and Shawty Redd, respectively.

"I don't even like to refer to it as Trap music," Jeezy admitted. "I just feel like it's the voice of the people, man. It was about the hunger and the struggle. We were just tired of taking 'no' for an answer and we just had to figure out our own way. We [Atlanta rappers] weren't big in New York then. We had to make enough noise for them to come down here and feel us. That's why it started because we gave them the real, we gave them what mattered, and they considered it to be Trap music because it was from the streets."

Trap History

CHAPTER VII

GUCCI MANE: THE PLUG TO TRAP MUSIC STARDOM

Gucci Mane

Three weeks before the release of his critically-acclaimed album *The State vs. Radric Davis*, Radric Davis sat in a barber's chair and reminisced about a time before the world knew him as Gucci Mane. While preparing for a photoshoot, he talked about the years which followed his mother's relocation from his grandfather's home at 1017 First Avenue in Bessemer, Alabama to the East Atlanta community of Atlanta, Georgia.

East Atlanta is one of the most historic areas in Georgia. During the Civil War, it was the location of the deadly Battle of Atlanta which led to Union soldiers overtaking the Confederate Army. Mostly segregated following the Civil War, East Atlanta remained a coveted community up until the late 1960s when white flight occurred. The abandonment of homes and businesses in the area coincided with an influx of crime during the 1980s and '90s. That same crime element would take hold of a young Gucci Mane as he would later share his experiences of life in East Atlanta through music.

At the age of 9, Gucci Mane and his family initially lived at the extended-stay motel Knights Inn located on Bouldercrest Road. They would settle at the Mountain Park Apartments and eventually found a place to stay in the Sun Valley Apartments.

With his mother working several jobs to make ends meet, Gucci Mane found ways to make money on his own. He would often empty his neighbors' trash to earn a dollar or two as a kid, and his first official job was bagging groceries at a Wayfield Foods supermarket on Bouldercrest Road. During his mid-teens, the Trap became his place of employment.

"When I was in the Trap, I would get up early in the morning and be out on the corner before everybody," Gucci Mane recalled while getting his haircut. "And I would stay out there later than anyone. I did the same thing with rap. I'd get up at 9 or 10 a.m. and record for twelve or thirteen hours. Sometimes I would be there for days sleeping in the studio. I'd work it like the dope game."

Gucci Mane graduated from McNair High School in 1998 with a 3.0 GPA and earned the HOPE Scholarship as a freshman at Georgia Perimeter College, a two-year state school at the time. But he would leave Georgia Perimeter College after being arrested on drug charges. He eventually turned to rap, first working as a manager for a teenaged rapper named Lil Buddy.

Through a mutual friend, Gucci Mane discovered a barber who produced beats in his mother's basement. He took Lil Buddy to the studio operated by Xavier Dotson, later known as Zaytoven, a church-going musician who had recently moved to Atlanta from San Francisco, California.

While in their first studio session, Zaytoven noticed that Gucci Mane would write lyrics for Lil Buddy and often coach him on how to rap the lyrics. Zaytoven saw the potential in Gucci Mane early and encouraged him to start rapping. Although he would often freestyle with friends while living in the Sun Valley Apartments, Gucci Mane never desired to be a rapper. But after Lil Buddy became distracted and quit music, Gucci Mane was left with a slew of beats he purchased from Zaytoven for $1,000. After serving a sixty-day sentence in jail, Gucci Mane decided to try his hand at rap.

Along with his collaborations with Zaytoven, Gucci Mane also began to work with producer Albert Alan who was once a keyboardist for Silk, an R&B group that garnered fame in the early 1990s. In 2001, Gucci Mane released his first independent project, *Str8 Drop Records Present Gucci Mane La Flare*. Only one thousand copies were released, but even small success inspired him to aim bigger in terms of rap.

Gucci Mane's first big break in rap came with the song "Black Tee" in 2004, a song initially released by him and members of Str8 Drop. "Black Tee" was a parody and more sinister version of Dem Franchize Boyz' hit, "White Tee." The remix featured Lil Scrappy, Bun B, Killer Mike, Jody Breeze, and Jeezy.

Following the buzz of "Black Tee," Gucci Mane and Jeezy would meet for the first time near Walter's Clothing, a renowned sneaker and athletic store located in downtown Atlanta. They both exchanged each other's music and agreed to record together in a session at Patchwerk Recording Studios.

Their first recording session at Patchwerk got off to a slow start as neither artists could agree on a beat or song. Gucci Mane decided to call Zaytoven, who was cutting hair at the time and invite him to the session.

Zaytoven made his way to the West Midtown, Atlanta studio and played several instrumentals from a beat CD. Gucci Mane picked an instrumental that would serve as the sound behind his first hit, "Icy." Jeezy would add a rap verse, Dungeon Family's crooner Lil Will sung the hook, and the song would become one of the biggest hits of 2005.

The commercial success of "Icy" proved that Gucci Mane and Jeezy were the next rap stars from Atlanta to capture the spotlight. By the spring of 2005, both artists were the most coveted rookies in rap. T.I.'s Grand Hustle label would be the first to offer Gucci Mane a record deal, and the major labels followed in pursuit. Atlantic Records, Warner Bros., Universal Records, and Motown all offered Gucci Mane a deal based on the momentum behind "Icy." However, he eventually signed his first recording contract with Big Cat Records, an independent label owned by Marlon Rowe which also signed rappers Maceo and Rasheeda (Rasheeda would later star on the VH-1 reality TV show, "Love and Hip Hop Atlanta").

Big Cat records offered Gucci Mane a 50/50 partnership, a money advance, and the label reimbursed him for the money he spent producing his music as an independent artist. The deal also featured a clause where his LaFlare Entertainment record label would receive distribution through Tommy Boy Records in a joint venture.

Gucci Mane's career appeared to be on the rise. However, a disagreement that began in the recording booth would linger into the streets and eventually turn violent.

The song "Icy" appeared on Jeezy's seminal mixtape, *Trap or Die*, but his record label, Def Jam, could not secure the song for his debut album, *Let's Get It: Thug Motivation 101*. Gucci Mane and Big Cat records decided to keep the song exclusive for Gucci's *Trap House* album which was scheduled to be released two months before Jeezy's debut album. Both artists agreed to shoot a video for "Icy," but their issues with each other came to light following the release of diss records such as "Stay Strapped" by Jeezy and "Round One" by Gucci Mane. Within weeks of releasing diss records, the beef between Jeezy and Gucci Mane would reach a boiling point.

On a warm night in May of 2005, Gucci Mane and a friend decided to visit a woman at her home in Decatur, Georgia. The woman worked as a stripper at Blazin' Saddles, a shoddy strip club located in an obscure section of Moreland Avenue where most of the scenery consisted of truck stops, used tires shops, and warehouses. Gucci Mane and a male friend met with the woman at her home which existed on a dead-end street called Springside Run. He wanted to play a few songs for the woman with the hopes that she would give it to a DJ at Blazin' Saddles. Within minutes of Gucci and his friend walking inside of the home, their meeting took a tragic turn.

Four armed men reportedly dressed in all-black, kicked down the woman's front door. The men aimed guns at Gucci Mane, tied him up, and pistol-whipped his friend. At some point, Gucci Mane was able to break free and wrestled a gun away from one of the attackers. He fired shots at the men as they ran from the woman's home.

Several days later, the body of Henry Lee Clark III, 27, was found in a wooded area near Columbia Middle School. Clark was reportedly an associate of Jeezy and a rapper known as Pookie Loc. According to multiple reports, Jeezy did not have any involvement with the break-in or shooting. Days before the scheduled release of his debut album, *Trap House*, Gucci Mane faced murder charges.

While in New York promoting his album on BET's "Rap City," Gucci Mane discovered that he would be charged with a crime that could change his life forever.

After driving thirteen hours from New York to Atlanta, Gucci Mane turned himself in to authorities at the Dekalb County Jail. A sea of reporters stood outside of the jail as Gucci Mane arrived with his lawyer. While wearing a T-shirt with a picture of Dr. Martin Luther King, Jr., Gucci Mane remained silent as reporters asked questions about the home invasion and murder. If convicted, Gucci Mane would face life in prison.

While dealing with the murder charge, Gucci Mane also faced a charge from an incident where he allegedly assaulted a man with a pool stick at Big Cat's studio. He was arrested while out on bail and booked into the Fulton County Jail.

Commonly known by Atlantans as Rice Street jail, nicknamed after the dead-end street where it exists, the Fulton County Jail was often an overcrowded facility that housed the most hardened criminals in the city. Those charged with murder, kidnapping, or rape in

Fulton County usually awaited their trial or sentencing at the Fulton County Jail.

Within a month of being locked up in the Fulton County Jail, Gucci Mane nearly caught another murder charge after a brutal fight left an inmate unconscious. The dispute began after the inmate approached Gucci Mane from behind and hit him with a large metal object. Gucci Mane turned the tables on the inmate, punched him repeatedly, and nearly threw him down a set of stairs. An older inmate who witnessed the fight urged Gucci Mane to think twice before causing further harm to the man. Gucci Mane, who lost a tooth during the rumble, decided to put the unconscious man down and spent the next three months in solitary confinement.

He would remain in jail until the end of 2005, but Gucci Mane began to see a glimmer of hope by the start of 2006. His lawyers were able to find an eyewitness to the home invasion who supported Gucci Mane's claim of self-defense. Due to insufficient evidence, the Dekalb County district attorney's office dropped the murder charges. He also resolved the assault charge by agreeing to pay his victim's medical bills. Gucci Mane would be released from jail within days of the start of 2006.

Over the next decade, Gucci Mane would continue to find himself in constant trouble with the law, and he also developed an addiction to ecstasy pills, and lean (Promethazine and Sprite).

But Gucci Mane's unrelenting work ethic allowed him to stand out in music at a time of severe turmoil in his real life. He would submerge himself in the studio for weeks at a time, churning out songs as if he was mass-producing Trap music on an assembly line. Following his 2005 debut *Trap House*, Gucci Mane released over eighty mixtapes and albums in twelve years. Standout mixtapes included the *Trap God* series with DJ Scream; *Chicken Talk* with DJ Burn One; and *The Burrrrptint* with DJ Drama.

Most of Gucci Mane's songs were created at his home studio, Brick Factory, located in East Atlanta. I visited Brick Factory for the first time in March of 2013. At the time, Brick Factory was similar to a boot camp for up-and-coming Trap music artists. O.J. da Juiceman, Rich Homie Quan, and Young Scooter were all present at the studio alongside Gucci Mane on the day I entered the Brick Factory. Young Scooter had recently released the song "Colombia," which would become a regional hit and later gained traction on the Billboard charts. On that day, I interviewed Young Scooter who spoke about the song and his relationship with Gucci Mane.

"I didn't think 'Colombia' was a hit until Gucci told me it was a hit," Young Scooter shared with me. "I later realized it was a hit when the streets and strip clubs picked it up."

Gucci Mane, shirtless with several diamond-encrusted chains hanging from his neck, nodded his head in agreement with Young Scooter's answers, but he mostly remained quiet during the interview. Like a point guard dishing out an assist or a coach prepping a young player, I noticed that Gucci Mane could take a step back to allow others to shine. He knew the potential and had a way of cultivating a new generation of

Trap music artists. When it came to discovering talent, Gucci Mane stood as the plug to Trap music stardom.

THE PLUG TO TRAP MUSIC STARDOM

Future: In the spring of 2011, Future was still building his name outside of Atlanta. Most knew him as Meathead, the cousin of Dungeon Family's Rico Wade. Meathead would eventually change his name to Future and scored a feature on YC's hit single "Racks" which was followed by the release of his solo hit single, "Tony Montana." Both songs received national radio play and eventually led to Future signing a deal with Epic Records after initially being signed to Rocko's A1 Records. Gucci Mane would collaborate with Future on his first prominent mixtape, *Free Bricks*, released in the summer of 2011.

Young Thug: By 2012, Young Thug generated a respectable buzz in Atlanta after releasing the third installment of his independent mixtape series *I Came from Nothing*. Atlanta rapper Pee Wee Longway initially introduced Young Thug to Gucci Mane in 2013. Without hearing a song, Gucci Mane gave Young Thug $25,000 and signed him to his 1017 Records label. Young Thug eventually released the acclaimed *1017 Thug* mixtape series and several Gucci Mane collaborations before releasing the gold-selling singles, "Stoner" and "Danny Glover" in 2014.

2 Chainz: Ludacris, and business partner Shaka

Zulu, can be credited for signing Tity Boi to Disturbing Tha Peace records during his days with the group, Playaz Circle. But by 2011, Tity Boi rebranded himself as 2 Chainz and garnered attention as a solo artist. Two years prior, 2 Chainz was featured on Gucci Mane's *Writings on the Wall* mixtape and his 2012 offering *Trap Back*.

Rich Homie Quan: Rich Homie Quan exploded in rap in the summer of 2013 after the release of his first major hit "Type of Way." But three months before that single hit, Rich Homie Quan was featured on three songs from Gucci Mane's *Trap House III* album.

Mike Will Made-It: In 2005, Mike Will Made-It was a young producer selling beats for only $100 per track. But that year, he had a chance encounter with Gucci Mane that would change his life forever. While with a friend at the renowned Patchwerk Studio in Atlanta, Mike Will Made-It bumped into Gucci Mane, who was working on music. Mike introduced himself to Gucci and told him that he produced it. Gucci Mane took Mike's beat CD, wrote a rap the same day, and offered him $1,000 on the spot for the beat. Gucci Mane would eventually give Mike his moniker with the lyric "Mike Will made it, Gucci Mane slayed it" on the song "Star Status." Mike and Gucci would continue to collaborate, but Mike also produced top hits for artists such as Beyoncé, Rihanna, Kendrick Lamar, and Future. Mike Will Made-It partnered with Interscope Records for his EarDrummers Records label in 2013 and signed successful acts such as Rae Sremmurd and

Trouble.

Metro Boomin: Before entering his senior year in high school, Metro Boomin found a unique summer job. After uploading beats online, the St. Louis-raised producer connected with Gucci Mane's protégé OJ da Juiceman and found himself producing in Atlanta. While enrolled at Morehouse College, Gucci Mane used Metro Boomin's beat for the song, "Pull Up On Ya," featured on the album *The State vs. Radric Davis II*. Metro Boomin would become a trusted producer for Future, Migos, Young Thug, and 21 Savage. He produced Future's hit single, "Mask Off."

Migos: In 2013, Migos shed light on how abandoned homes in the Atlanta area would become prime locations for drug activity with their single "Bando." Gucci Mane favored the song after Zaytoven showed him the video on YouTube and he soon began working with the group. Migos collaborated with Gucci Mane on the song "Dennis Rodman," and they later released an entire mixtape with Gucci Mane called *The Green Album*. Migos would sign with Gucci Mane's close friend, Pierre Thomas, who formed the Quality Control record label with Coach K.

Waka Flocka: Following his jail stint in 2006, Gucci Mane was introduced to Deb Antney by Jacob York. Antney helped Gucci Mane with his community service efforts and would later introduce him to Jimmy Henchmen, who facilitated his release from Big Cat Records and helped to broker his deal with Atlantic Records. Antney's son, Waka Flocka, would develop a close bond with Gucci Mane and the two formed a group called the Ferrari Boyz following the success of Waka Flocka's debut, *Flockaveli*. But Gucci Mane's relationship with Waka Flocka and Antney soured as they became entangled by lawsuits against each other and a war of words. In his book, *The Autobiography of Gucci Mane*, the rapper wrote that Atlanta producer Polow Da Don initially saw Waka Flocka as a star who Gucci Mane could mold. Waka Flocka would later say that his mother Deb Antney deserved most of the credit for his career. Their feud hindered the prospect of future collaborations for years, but no one could deny their strong run together from 2009 until 2012. In November of 2018, Waka Flocka expressed his interest in squashing his beef with Gucci Mane in a video he posted on his Instagram page. One month later, Gucci Mane revealed in an interview with Atlanta radio station Streetz 945 that he and Waka Flocka finally spoke and decided to move past their beef.

Other notable artists to collaborate with Gucci Mane early in their careers include Ralo, Hood Rich Pablo Juan, Young Dolph, Young Scooter, Bankroll Fresh, Peewee Longway, and Pooh Shiesty and the New 1017. Gucci Mane would also team up with Miss Mulatto (Big Latto) for the song "Muwop."

After a series of arrests for battery and assault, Gucci Mane pleaded guilty to a charge of possession of a firearm in 2014. He was sentenced to three years in federal prison.

While Gucci Mane served time at Terre Haute prison in Indiana, the sound created by Atlanta artists and producers became dominant in every region of hip-hop.

Young Thug, Offset, and Young Scooter would later pay homage to Gucci Mane with the song "Guwop." In an interview, Young Thug shared with me how Gucci Mane inspired him musically.

During a muggy summer day in June of 2015, Young Thug walked into Studio 2B located near Atlantic Station alongside his fianceé, Jerrika Karlae. I interviewed them both for a cover story that was published a few weeks after our meeting. Standing at 6-foot-3, Young Thug commanded the entire room while saying very few words. Dressed in a red leather jacket and white jeans, Young Thug's style was reminiscent of rock stars such as Jimi Hendrix or, possibly, Motley Crue. At the time, Young Thug was somewhat of an enigma in rap. His lyrics were often fast-paced, indecipherable, and reminiscent of jazz era scat singing. But his raps also possessed an intoxicating quality, mostly due to his high-pitched voice which produced a sound unlike anything heard in rap.

We discussed his upbringing in the Jonesboro South housing projects in South Atlanta, growing up in a household with ten other siblings, and his rise in music. We also talked about his relationship with Gucci Mane and his influence on a new generation of rappers.

"Gucci and I are from the same set," Young Thug shared. "Gucci is going to make you a man. Gucci is going to make you a monster. Gucci is going to make you rich. Gucci is going to make you share. It's hard to believe, too. He gave my partner some money. I've always been a sharing person. But he made me keep going because at one point, I was on the verge of not doing shit for anybody because nobody was doing anything for me. But I'll hear him say nobody does anything for him and that he does everything for everybody. But he still gives."

Days before Memorial Day 2016, Gucci Mane became a free man. After serving three years at Terre Haute Federal Correctional Institution on drug and gun charges, he emerged from prison. Still confined to house arrest, Gucci Mane set up a makeshift studio in his Atlanta area home and began recording. Six days later, he completed an entire album.

Gucci Mane promoted the release of the album *Everybody Looking* on the night of July 22, 2016. Before a capacity crowd at Atlanta's Fox Theater, Gucci Mane performed his first concert following his release from prison. Artists such as Drake, Future, and 2 Chainz all served as guest performers at a show that had the feel of a homecoming celebration. Gucci Mane had waited a decade to experience that night.

Although Gucci Mane released notable hit songs and albums before his incarceration, he had yet to experience the mainstream success that his Trap counterparts T.I. and Jeezy captured early in their careers. Even when signed to a major record label, Gucci Mane maintained the aura of an independent artist. He rarely collaborated with pop artists, save for his 2009 collaboration with Mariah Carey on the song "Obsessed," or appeared on mainstream TV shows such as "Saturday Night Live" or "The Tonight Show." Gucci Mane became a staple within urban communities but was far from being a household name before his stint in prison.

But several things occurred during his incarceration that elevated his status to the mainstream. The day Gucci Mane was arrested in 2013, the next generation of Trap music artists and producers began to take over the scene. The success of Migos, Future, 2 Chainz, Young Thug, Mike-Will Made It, and Metro Boomin kept Gucci Mane's story alive. The young artists and producers who were inspired by his sound and flow allowed his style to remain relevant. It allowed Gucci Mane to become one of rap's mythical figures.

Gucci Mane emerged from prison with a more slim and refined look. His homecoming concert on that warm summer night in July 2016 represented a new beginning. He gave credit to his then-fiancée, now wife, Keyshia Ka'oir, for helping him make the transition. She encouraged him to work out more, follow a schedule, and eat healthier foods. The gut that once overlapped his waistband was gone. He smiled from ear to ear as if he had never encountered a stressful day in life. Gucci Mane was prepared to embrace his second act.

With rap being a music genre that is fueled by newness and youth, Gucci Mane's late success can be considered an anomaly. Ten years following the release of his debut album, he finally entered the mainstream. At the age of 36, Gucci Mane was heading toward the zenith of his career.

THE INVENTOR OF TRAP MUSIC?

On the first week of April 2018, Gucci Mane posted a photo on Instagram with a caption that sparked a heated debate involving Trap music. The photo, circa 2005, featured Gucci Mane in a white fur coat standing in front of a white hummer with the caption, "The Day I Invented Trap Music."

Days later, T.I. would respond to Gucci Mane's post on Instagram with the caption, "Ok, so again for the slow ones in the back. August 19, 2003 birth of *Trap Muzik* and only fools dispute facts." T.I. wrote.

The debate continued online as social media users argued over who should hold the title as the inventor of Trap music. I decided to get quotes from several artists on the subject, including Killer Mike and Zaytoven.

"There's no debate about Trap music," Killer Mike told me in May 2018. "The first person to say Trap music as a genre was T.I. He and DJ Toomp created a subgenre within hip-hop called Trap music, trap music has been done well and perfected by a lot of people. From Jeezy to Guwop. Many people said that word Trap before because it's an Atlanta word. I said it in raps, OutKast said it, Goodie Mob said it, Backbone said it. But shout out to T.I. and DJ Toomp had the foresight and vision to make Trap music an actual thing."

In June 2018, Zaytoven responded to the debate by telling me, "There is a difference in sound." Zaytoven continued, "Some people would debate and come to me and say, 'Zay, you and Gucci started Trap music.' I came from the Bay Area, and I didn't know what the word Trap meant. I knew T.I. had an album called *Trap Muzik* and Jeezy had a mixtape called *Trap or Die*. But I think the sound that the world knows as Trap music right now is the sound Gucci and I created. That is the sound being mimicked til this day. When I heard

Migos 'Bando,' that's the same Gucci sound. When you hear Young Dolph, that's the same sound that was created when I was working with Gucci. That sound came from me being impatient and not taking the time to learn my equipment.

There are certain things you need to change when you're using 808 drums on the MPC to make it sound right. When you got a guy like Gucci who is ready to go in the studio and rap, I didn't have time to change the velocity to make it sound right. I would just put the beat on and let him rap. The way we work, we're doing ten songs per day. So we didn't [always] have time to fix it, we would just keep recording and put it out. That became the sound. It was rough. The 808 drums would bleed on top of each other, the piano would be too low, the snare drums may be too high, it was all over the place. And when Gucci rapped, sometimes he would rap too fast on the beat and some people didn't understand it. The songs being rough made it authentic Trap music. It's not something that's been mixed well. I think that's the reason why the Trap music that we made has been so popular. It's spontaneous. It's how we feel right now. We want it to feel rough so when you hear it, it sounds like it was recorded in someone's basement."

The discussion over who invented Trap music proved to be great fodder for social media users, music journalists, and bloggers. But the debate alone revealed the power of the genre. It was a genre that had become so big that it could never be minimized by one voice, one style, or one sound.

CHAPTER VIII

HOW MIGOS' *CULTURE* ALBUM CHANGED THE CULTURE OF TRAP MUSIC

Offset of Migos

Takeoff of Migos

Quavo of Migos

In 2012, Kevin Lee, known in the music industry as Coach K, took a road trip to Gwinnett County, Georgia. The nearly forty-five-minute drive north of the city of Atlanta could be a nuisance considering that traffic on Interstate 85 was often at a standstill. But the possibility of bad traffic did not deter the man who once managed the careers of artists such as Jeezy and Gucci Mane. That drive would become one of the most significant road trips in Coach K's life.

Once he made it to Gwinnett County, Coach K knocked on the door of a home owned by Edna Marshall, the mother of Quavious Marshall. Edna advised Coach K and his assistant to walk around to a side door. After walking through patches of mud, he entered a basement and saw a computer that sat on top of a chair, a makeshift recording booth, and a blanket covering the recording booth with a microphone in it. The homemade studio was a sign of ambition, but the quality of the songs that were made in that studio proved to be a sign of promise. This was Coach K's introduction to the Migos.

The three-man group Migos consisted of Quavo, Offset (Kiari Cephus), and Takeoff (Kirshnik Ball). They are all related with Quavo being Takeoff's uncle and Offset is Quavo's cousin. During their teen years,

Quavo stood out as a star quarterback at Berkmar High School. The school's football team only won one game during Quavo's senior year, but he set a Gwinnett County record for most completions in a football game with twenty-nine in 2009.

Quavo would leave school after the football season to pursue music full-time with his group, then known as Polo Club. Recording in the basement studio they called the bando, the group would change their name to Migos before releasing their debut mixtape *Jugg Season* in the summer of 2011. At the top of 2012, Migos released their sophomore mixtape *No Label* which featured their first viral hit, "Bando."

Bando is a slang term for an abandoned house or apartment. In some areas in Atlanta, a multitude of abandoned homes became locations where drug deals and other crimes took place.

Zaytoven produced the music behind the song "Bando," however; he initially did not know that Migos recorded the song over his track until after it began to gain a substantial amount of views on YouTube.

"I got popular by giving out beats throughout the city," Zaytoven revealed. "I may have a CD with forty beats. I may give you a beat CD, and you may record to six of them. Migos, Young Scooter, and Future were all rapping over my beats, but I did not know where they got them from. Young LA came to my house and told me,'these rappers are rapping over your beat and they're going so crazy.' I started searching for the Migos [online]. Once I heard [the song], I knew I had to find them."

During a studio session with Gucci Mane, Zaytoven

played the "Bando" video on YouTube. Impressed by the music, Gucci Mane called the booking info in their bio and invited the trio to his studio, the Brick Factory. With Offset in jail in DeKalb County on a probation violation, Quavo and Takeoff were the two who represented the group during their first meeting with Gucci Mane.

Following the meeting, Gucci Mane would call Miss Rici, an Atlanta-based manager and booking agent who had previously worked with artists such as Gucci Mane and Wale. Miss Rici shared with me how she initially began to promote the Migos.

"I was in New York with Wale and Gucci called and told me he had these guys who he wanted me to work with," Miss Rici told me during an interview. "When I got back to Atlanta, [I met] Takeoff, Quavo, and [their manager] Rel. We would talk to Offset over the phone [while he was in jail]. Gucci would always say, 'the one in jail is hard.' I set up their interviews with V-103 and Greg Street."

Miss Rici was instrumental in helping to introduce the Migos to the media. But as they began to brand the group, Gucci Mane was sentenced to prison. Migos would eventually sign with Coach K and Pierre "Pee" Thomas after the industry veterans created Quality Control Music.

In the summer of 2013, Migos would receive their first significant break with the release of the song "Versace." Produced by Zaytoven, the Migos introduced a unique style of rapping known as the triplet rhyme scheme.

The triplet rhyme scheme stands out because the

rapper rhymes three notes in a timeframe that would usually call for two notes. Rappers start the triplet rhyme scheme by mimicking the beat with the first note, moving quickly ahead to the second note, and returning on the beat by the third note. Because most Trap beats are produced with snare rolls and heavy 808 drums, the triplet rhyme scheme often turns the voice into an additional instrument that coincides perfectly with drum patterns used. Rhyming in triplets can also force listeners to be more attentive because it can sound as if more words are being offered in a less amount of time.

"Think when the Migos came out, every rapper started sounded like them," Coach K shared during a keynote speech at Morehouse College in 2018. "That's one of the reasons we named the album *Culture* because they shifted and changed the culture of music. The cadence and style. It was the biggest shift ever."

Migos can be credited for introducing the triplet rhyme scheme to the Trap music era and, in a way, inspiring artists such as Jay-Z, Drake, and Kanye West who also used the rhyme scheme following the release of Migos' hits "Versace" and "Hannah Montana." Artists such as Chuck D, Lord Infamous, T Rock, and Intoxicated of Big Oomp Records flirted with the triplet rhyme scheme years before the ascension of Trap music.

"Versace" began as a regional hit in the South, but it became a national hit when Drake jumped on the remix. The trio met Drake for the first time during the annual Birthday Bash concert in Atlanta in 2014.

"I introduced them to Drake at Birthday Bash," Miss Rici shared with me. "Drake said that he heard the 'Bando' song. They took a picture that night and Drake jumped on the 'Versace' remix a few days after. I knew the [Migos] was going to be who they are because they had that energy."

Migos put out eleven mixtapes before the release of their official debut album *Yung Rich Nation* in the summer of 2015. The group garnered a respectable buzz after the song "Look At My Dab" inspired a dance that went viral as NFL players such as Cam Newton and Julio Jones did the dance after scoring touchdowns. But Migos would become solidified stars in music following the release of the Metro Boomin-produced song, "Bad & Bougie," in October 2016.

On January 7, 2017, Donald Glover accepted the Golden Globe Award for "Atlanta," which won Best Television Series, Musical or Comedy. The TV show takes a comedic, and at times dramatic, look at Atlanta's hip-hop scene, the nuances of the city, and the everyday people who exist in it. In the TV series on FX, Glover stars as Earn, an Ivy League dropout looking to find himself by latching onto the talents of his cousin, Alfred "Paper Boi," played by Brian Tyree, who scored a local radio hit. The two are accompanied by Darius, played by LaKeith Stanfield, Alfred's roommate, and eccentric friend. On their quest for fame, the trio lives hustle-to-hustle, finding different ways to make a few dollars when a chance presents itself.

Glover thanked Migos for making the song "Bad and Boujee" during his acceptance speech. For many of the Hollywood elite, it was their first introduction to Migos and Trap music. Glover's speech led to a two hundred and forty-three percent increase in Spotify streams for "Bad & Bougie" and, arguably, catapulted the Migos into the mainstream. It became one of the first rap songs that proved Trap music had become popular music. Two weeks after Glover's speech, Migos released the *Culture* album and it topped the Billboard 200 charts in its first week of release. They would follow-up with another number one album, *Culture II*, in 2018 and each member would release solo projects in the months that followed.

Migos proved to be another example of how Trap music could begin in a bando and work its way to mainstream success.

"Trap is international. It's a global movement," Quavo of Migos said during an interview in 2016. "It's fun and energetic. It's young and new. This is a new wave. This is a new generation. It's culture everywhere. It's bigger than just Migos, it's culture around the world. We had fun in Africa. It was a great experience to see that they knew every word and it was our first time being there."

Quavo's partner Offset echoed his sentiments by adding, "It's cool to see that others look up to us or are influenced by what we are doing. It's positive to be able to influence people. When it comes to rap in general everyone is straight out of Atlanta."

The success of Migos coincided with the success of the independent record label, Quality Control. With guidance from label owners Coach K and Pierre Thomas, Quality Control also signed successful acts such as Lil Yachty, Lil Baby, the Miami-based female duo, City Girls, and Lil Marlo. Unfortunately, Lil Marlo, whose real name is Rudolph Johnson, was shot and killed while driving on I-285 in Atlanta on July 12, 2020. He had recently released the mixtape, *1st & 3rd*. Lil Marlo, a father of two, was only 30 years old.

THE ART OF MUMBLE RAP

The Migos, along with artists such as Future, Young Thug, and 21 Savage, faced criticism from some who found their lyrics indecipherable. In an attempt to dismiss Southern rap, some critics took aim by calling thier music, "mumble rap."

Mumble rap would serve as a punching bag and symbol of hip-hop's generational and regional divide. To some who considered themselves hip-hop purists, mumble rap represented everything that was wrong with the present and future of hip-hop.

But in a sense, those artists used music to share how they spoke with their peers in Atlanta. Mumble rap essentially presented a Southern conversation through music.

There is a rhythm and soulfulness to Southern dialect. When set to music, Atlanta's mumbled dialect becomes art. Atlanta-based rappers and producers thrived by remaining true to the city's sound and culture. So when a few rappers began to "mumble" over beats, they were remaining true to their experiences. Mumble rap can also be viewed as a form of coded language. Coded language and slang have remained essential to blacks in America since slavery. What began as a tool for misdirection and survival eventually became a key element of black culture and music.

From scat singing in jazz to James Brown's soulful grunts, black artists have always experimented with lyrics and sounds. If there is room to disparage some songs for lacking a traditional direction, there should also be room to view mumble rap as an extension to musical experimentation.

PART II: THE TRAP

CHAPTER
VIX

WELCOME TO THE BLUFF: AMERICA'S MOST NOTORIOUS TRAP

Dilapedated apartment complex in the Bluff.

Trap History

In the Bluff, Atlanta's glistening city skyline can be seen in the near distance. It's about half a mile away from the Atlanta University Center and within walking distance of the $1 billion home of the Atlanta Falcons, the Mercedes-Benz Stadium.

A number of the shotgun homes in the Bluff consisted of windows and doors that were covered by wooden boards. Front yards became lots where beer bottles, fast food containers, and drug syringes were the only evidence that life did exist in some nearby capacity. More than a few of the abandoned homes served as makeshift drug houses, also known as Trap houses, where users shot heroin until they nodded off, lying dormant on bare floors until their bodies yearned for the next hit.

In broad daylight, drug dealers occupied street corners as drug users roamed through the neighborhood searching for ways to get a hit of heroin, cocaine, or crack. Dealers in the Bluff referred to heroin as "boy" and often threw sample bags of new product on the streets for users to test on Sunday mornings.

The allure of good dope transcended race in the Bluff. In a community where the residents were predominately black, it was common to see white drug users drive slowly through the neighborhood searching for their next fix. Once they bought heroin or cocaine, their cars sped away from the blighted Hell they were lucky to be able to escape. But for some residents, escape remained impossible. The Bluff engulfed everything around it like a black hole waiting to claim its next victim.

Kathryn Johnston, a 92-year-old grandmother, became an unfortunate casualty of the Bluff. On a Tuesday evening one week before Thanksgiving 2006, Atlanta Police Department officers, Jason Smith, Gregg Junnier, and Arthur Tesler approached Johnston's home with guns drawn in search of a suspect who reportedly had a kilogram of cocaine.

Earlier that day, the officers arrested Fabian Sheets in the Bluff and planted a bag of marijuana on him, threatening to arrest him unless he could offer information about drug transactions in the Bluff. The suspect sensed the officers' desperation and decided to use it against them to free himself. He described to the officers how he bought crack cocaine from a guy named Sam and noticed a kilogram of cocaine inside of the home. Sheets took the officers to a location that they believed was owned by Sam. With Sheets' information, the officers finally scored the tip they desired. All they would need was a confidential informant to admit to purchasing drugs from the home to obtain a search warrant.

But instead of setting up a sting with a confidential informant or further investigating the property for drug activity, the police officers went to the Fulton County jail and drafted an affidavit with false information that detailed a drug purchase. The officers were eventually able to convince a magistrate judge to issue a "no-knock" warrant, thus allowing them to enter the home with brute force without revealing their identities.

Catching a prominent drug dealer often paved the way for officers to receive promotions and other bonuses. It also allowed officers to seize valuables through the civil assets forfeiture law. Through the law, officers could seize money, cars, and homes from individuals if presumed that the items were used or purchased as a result of a crime. The police officers believed that any drug dealer who could buy a $30,000 kilogram of cocaine was sure to have thousands of dollars in his possession.

Shortly before 7 p.m. that evening, officers approached Johnston's home with narcotics officers in tow. Tesler positioned himself in the back of the house as Smith pried open the metal burglar bars on the front door. Smith kicked down the door and barged inside with Junnier and the narcotics officers.

A single gunshot was fired in the direction of the front door as the officers rushed inside, but the bullet hit no one. The officers reacted by firing thirty-nine shots. When the smoke finally cleared, 92-year-old Kathryn Johnston was lying motionless in a pool of her blood. Without attempting to apply CPR to Johnston, officer Smith handcuffed the dead woman and searched the home for drugs and other occupants.

Officers Smith, Junnier, and Tesler were responsible for murdering an innocent woman and looking for ways to hide their crime. Smith placed the same marijuana he found earlier in the woods in the basement of

Johnston's home; Junnier drafted a false police report that stated a drug purchase was made at the house earlier that day, and they attempted to have a confidential informant lie about purchasing drugs from the home.

But there were no other occupants in the home, there was no kilogram of cocaine, and "Sam" the drug dealer did not exist. The officers were responsible for murdering a black woman who lived through the Great Depression, Jim Crow, both world wars and Vietnam, and the Civil Rights Movement.

They pleaded guilty to federal charges of conspiracy and civil rights violations. Tesler was sentenced to five years in prison, Junnier was sentenced to six years, and Smith received a ten-year sentence.

This type of greed and violence by law enforcement is often commonplace in black communities. It's highly unlikely that police would have killed Johnston had she lived in a more affluent neighborhood in Buckhead. Innocent residents are also victims when their homes exist in areas that become the Trap.

The Bluff gained some national attention with the 2011 independent film *Snow on tha Bluff*. Released on Netflix, the film follows a resident of the Bluff, Curtis Snow, as he navigates the streets of his neighborhood while raising his infant son. Shot docu-style, several scenes in *Snow on tha Bluff* depict graphic violence and drug abuse.

In one scene, Curtis Snow is filmed cutting what appears to be crack cocaine with a razor blade. His infant son sits on his lap as Snow separates the cocaine while at a table in his kitchen. That scene nearly led to a brawl during the opening night premiere of the film.

Snow on tha Bluff premiered for the first time at the Landmark Theatre in Midtown Atlanta on the night of May 2, 2011. It was an invite-only screening with journalists, tastemakers and influencers who were key figures in the city's entertainment industry. Curtis Snow and the film's producer, Damon Russell, were present with family and friends. When the scene of Snow cutting crack cocaine with his son appeared on the big screen, one moviegoer stood up, yelled profanities, and approached Snow and Russell. The moviegoer was appalled that the two would film a scene where an infant was inches away from crack cocaine, viewing it as irresponsible filmmaking. Snow and the upset moviegoer were both separated and escorted out of the theater before violence could erupt.

Snow would later admit to me that he used some level of shock value in the film to drive home a point. How could such dysfunction take place in a city known as the Black Mecca? How could that dysfunction be the reality for citizens in America?

"We just tried to bring you there in the middle of [the Bluff] and paint a picture," Snow would tell me in an interview. "It's a lot going on in our neighborhoods and cities that [people] know nothing about. We're trying to expose them to real poverty. It's going on right next door. If you have lived in Atlanta for a long time, you know how the city is run. I just wanted them to know the true story of Atlanta—behind the scenes. Slum neighborhoods still exist. This is more than a greeting card fairytale."

CHAPTER X

TRAPPED BY ADDICTION: TRAP MUSIC AND MENTAL HEALTH

On a sweltering afternoon in the Bluff during the summer of 2017, over one dozen people stood in line outside of a dull white Winnebago. The vehicle was parked on a street corner in front of the dilapidated St. Marks AME church. All that remained of the church was a grey cobblestone wall that covered a gutted interior. Dirt, rocks, and weeds replaced the church pews.

Three men in their late-forties to early-fifties were in front of the line dressed in shabby outfits. Their forearms were marked with scars and scabs. A guy in his mid-thirties with a low afro and scruffy beard stood behind the men. He appeared physically fit, but his eyes suggested the weariness of a man twice his age. A white couple in their mid-twenties were next in line. The male was sweating and a bit flustered as he held hands with his blonde-haired, blue-eyed girlfriend who had the youthful look of a college cheerleader. Bright red marks were on her lower left leg. The couple stood two places in front of a white woman in her mid-forties who clutched BMW car keys. Each person in line held a small brown paper or plastic bag. Once they were at the front of the line, they emptied their bags as used syringes fell into an open container. After signing a form, they were given new needles, rubber covers for crack pipes, cotton swabs, and condoms. This was a weekly process in the Bluff for individuals who were addicted to heroin or crack cocaine.

If there is an aspect that possibly gets lost within Trap music, it's the people who frequent the Trap due to addiction. Without prevalent drug addiction in specific communities, there would be no such thing as the Trap. But how do these individuals cope while struggling with drug abuse? I took a trip to the Bluff to get a glimpse of people who were trapped by addiction.

The Atlanta Harm Reduction Coalition has serviced the Bluff since 1994. The organization owns the dull-white Winnebago that provides new syringes and other items every Wednesday and Saturday afternoon for those who are addicted to drugs. The zip code where the Bluff exists (30318) has one of the highest HIV rates of any zip code in the state of Georgia. Many of the infections occur through the sharing of needles while shooting heroin. AHRC seeks to reduce those rates by performing outreach to drug users and providing education on HIV prevention. At the time, it was the state of Georgia's only needle exchange program.

One person who often made a weekly visit to the coalition's Winnebago is a man named Kareem. An unlit cigarette hung from the side of his mouth as he approached the Winnebago while riding a bike. Kareem's head was clean-shaven, and he wore a faded oversized shirt that covered his slender frame. His used needles were in a bag positioned near his bike's handlebars.

In his early fifties, Kareem was somewhat of a respected figure among the other drug users and coalition employees. He shook hands and greeted everyone, proudly showing a few missing teeth as he smiled from ear to ear. When two drug users began arguing over a position in line, Kareem stepped in between the two men and stopped them before the argument led to fisticuffs.

A lifetime resident of the neighborhood, Kareem lived in the Bluff when it was still mostly known as the English Avenue community, a place where middle-class blacks could find a home close to a burgeoning city on the rise. Dr. Martin Luther King, Jr. moved his family to a home in the English Avenue community during the 1960s. Located on Sunset Avenue, Dr. King's home represented the legacy of a community that fell shortly after the assassination of one of America's most revered leaders.

Kareem had been around long enough to witness the transition of the area from being noted as a place where Dr. King resided to being minimized to an acronym that represented an influx of poverty, crime, drugs, and hopelessness. He remembers earning good grades as a youth but being pulled by street life during his early teens. This was around the time his father left his family, leaving his mother to raise him and his five sisters on her own.

"By my mother being so focused on keeping my sisters together, I was able to slip out of the backdoor," Kareem admitted. "I learned how to shoot craps and shoot dope. In this community, drugs are a part of everyday life. You can sell it, use it, or do whatever you need with it."

Kareem began doing random crimes to support his drug addiction during his twenties. He found himself in and out of prison, and it became more challenging to kick his drug habit and find steady employment. "Atlanta has nothing to offer for an ex-felon," he said. "You can't get a job, and you can't even get a food stamp if you're an ex-felon. So what am I supposed to do? Starve? There isn't any human who would want to be sick and hungry. So you have to find any opportunity you can, whether it's legal or illegal."

When I met him, Kareem was at the point of his life where he felt as if dreams of a better situation could only be experienced when his eyes were closed. Years of drug abuse and constant incarceration stole the vitality and inspiration he once had during his youth. Although he retains an inkling of hope that he can overcome addiction while in the Bluff, he feels condemned to living the only life he has ever known.

"I don't want to be on drugs," Kareem told me. "I can really be a help to Atlanta if given the opportunity. I'm obligated to pass my experience down. A lot of the youth are upset because there is nothing for them to do, nowhere to go, no opportunities. They go to school, come back, and see dope selling and gangbanging. Pimps and hoes. It hurts me to see young sisters walking up the street hoeing. I've known them since they were in their mothers' stomachs. Now they're a lost hope. I'm fifty years old and I've been in the streets for close to thirty-five years. I'm ready to say 'No' to death and say 'Yes' to life. But where is the life? I don't see life in this community."

Kareem made his way to the front of the Winnebago where he exchanged his used needles for a bag of new syringes. He placed the bag of syringes on his bike's handlebars and peddled away. He waved to a man who stood near the vehicle. Before Kareem turned right on the next block, the man yelled to Kareem, "See you next week!"

Dressed in a crisp, clean white T-shirt and sporting an Atlanta Braves hat, the man who appeared to be in his early forties introduced himself as Gary. He decided to volunteer for the nonprofit organization after years of witnessing the deterioration of his neighborhood up close. In a sense, he's giving back some of what he may have taken away.

Gary was once the neighborhood dope man. He began selling crack cocaine in the Bluff at age fifteen. It was the mid-1990s and the drug game was at its peak in the Bluff. Gary described the area as a place primarily occupied by the users and dealers of drugs. If you were raised in the neighborhood at the time, according to Gary, there was a good chance that you were either selling or abusing drugs. Gary decided to become a dealer.

"My father gave me $300 and I decided to flip it," Gary recalled during our conversation. "A half (of an ounce of cocaine) would cost $500. I went to the dope man in the neighborhood and I gave him $300 and told him I would owe him $200. He gave me half and I cut it up. The first $200 I made, I gave it back to him. All of the rest of the profit was mine to keep. I made almost $1,000 off of his half. At that point, I was able to get more from him."

Gary became one of the more prominent drug dealers in the Bluff by his early twenties. "A Trap is just that, it's a Trap," he told me. "When I was selling drugs, I couldn't let people come sell in my territory. The word Trap means this is my area to sell. You can't sell your product over here."

Gary was confused by the notion presented in many rap songs that suggest every drug dealer is wealthy. Working in a drug Trap can be as much of a financial struggle as working in a fast-food restaurant. Most dealers only make around minimum wage when they begin selling drugs, and other occupational hazards abound that can prevent them from earning a life-changing income.

"It's not easy to sell drugs," Gary admitted. "Back in the day, you could make $500 a day out here. But money isn't out here like it used to be because people aren't in the Bluff. There are empty houses everywhere. You can make a Trap house, but there aren't people over here to buy. This neighborhood is gone. Some guys stand out here all day and only make $20. I remember we thought we were doing good when we made $1,000 in one day. But by the time you pay the bonding fee, the lawyer fee, and the commissary fee, every dollar you earned is gone. So you're back to where you started, broke."

Gary's fall in the drug game did not occur due to an arrest or lack of earning potential. He lost focus once he tried his own product.

"A girl turned me on to crack," Gary said, shaking his head in regret. "I knew what it could do, but I tried it. Some people start by smoking weed with their homeboys and then become weed addicts. Some will be at a nightclub and start sniffing coke at the club, and then become coke addicts. And they want another type of high and start smoking crack and shooting heroin. It happens. I was smoking weed and then started snorting powder cocaine. I was with a girl, and I had $1,800 worth of dope. She started smoking a geek joint, which is weed and crack cocaine. She started smoking it and kept pulling it. I wondered why she kept pulling it and I decided to try it out. I was hooked. She didn't force me into it, but she led me to this way."

Through drug counseling provided by a referral from AHRC, Gary said he remained clean from drugs for three years. He volunteered with AHRC during the needle exchange program in an attempt to help salvage what was left of a dying community.

"Everybody in that line is just trying to survive," Gary said, pointing at the individuals who were exchanging needles with AHRC. "They are all hooked on heroin, but some are just here to make an extra dollar. They get the new syringes and sell them. They flip the syringes and sell them for $3 a pop. It might be the only money they see all week."

The white woman who clutched the BMW car keys grabbed a bag of new syringes and walked swiftly to her vehicle without making direct eye contact with any person. Parked directly across the street from the coalition's Winnebago, the woman's black 5 Series BMW featured a license plate frame that read United BMW Roswell. Located north of Atlanta, the car dealership often serves clients who reside in the more affluent Alpharetta area, which is thirty miles north of the Bluff and English Avenue community. But when it comes to household income, education, and quality of life, the Bluff and Alpharetta may as well exist on different planets.

However, the woman's choice to drive a BMW alone into one of the most crime-ridden neighborhoods in Atlanta proves that there's a connection between the two locales. Regardless of race or class, the difficulties of addiction will never discriminate.

"We've seen an uptick in suburban zip codes who are coming to the Bluff," Mona Bennett, co-founder of the AHRC shared with me. "White people are driving in from Cobb County, Clayton County, Cherokee County, and Henry County. We're seeing more and more suburban zip codes. But what kind of pain are people in where they are needing to come to the Bluff, come to English Avenue, to try to find something to relieve that pain? What physical and mental issues are going undiagnosed and causing this self-medication? Let's start there. Georgia [lawmakers] have cracked down on pills in the last few years, so the pills are getting more expensive and are getting even harder to find. Well, that's when a $10 bag of heroin starts to look pretty darn good."

But as the face of drug abuse changed, the level of crime associated with it has changed also. When blacks were viewed as the primary drug abusers, legislation was created to place harsh jail sentences on the users and sellers of illegal drugs.

For decades, blacks were incarcerated at high rates for major and minor drug offenses. But once the heroin epidemic hit suburban America, there was a push to help instead of incarcerating those who were addicted.

I attended a speech given by President Barack Obama in 2016 where he discussed the racial dynamics of the drug war at the AmericasMart in Atlanta.

"Part of what has made it previously difficult to emphasize treatment over the criminal justice system has to do with the fact that the populations affected in the past were viewed as, or stereotypically identified as poor, minority, and as a consequence, the thinking was it is often a character flaw in those individuals who live in those communities, and it's not our problem they're just being locked up," President Obama said.

Bennett echoed President Obama's statement by revealing how race has changed the discussion when it comes to drugs, crime, and treatment.

"We didn't start seeing an emphasis on treatment or medical amnesty laws until it started affecting upper-middle-class white people," Bennett said. "Until then, the answer to drug use was lock them up. But now that more and more white people, especially those with political power, have friends and family who are being affected by addiction, well now it's time to slow the roll and make it kinder, gentler. So he [President Obama] is absolutely telling the truth. He could've went even further. Yes, race was the thing that is beginning to turn the conversations and the actions around addiction. Until then, it was lock up those people who don't matter anyway. But now that addiction is touching a whole lot of people who know their lawmakers, their policymakers by name, know how to write their Congresspeople, their elective representatives, now it's a different story. It's my job, and the job of the Atlanta Harm Reduction Coalition is to use that momentum to help everybody, and we will."

TRAP MUSIC AND MENTAL HEALTH

There was once a dope boy's doctrine that eschewed the use of hard drugs or any substance beyond marijuana. "Never get high on your own supply," became a common mantra in rap. The dealers were the dealers, and the users were the users.

However, the line between the drug dealer and the drug user became blurred in rap during the 2010s. In that era, rappers began to share stories of experimenting with drugs such as Xanax, Molly, and Percocet. In particular, Future had a way of making music which added allure to drug use.

With a sample from Tommy Butler's 1978 song "Prison Song," Metro Boomin produced "Mask Off" which was arguably the top rap song of 2017. "Prison Song" was featured on the soundtrack to *Selma The Musical*, a play that detailed the life of Dr. Martin Luther King, Jr. The sample of a melodic flute from "Prison Song" drove the production behind Future's "Mask Off." But it was Future's reference to the drugs Molly and Percocet which made "Mask Off" one of the most controversial drug endorsements in rap history. The song became Future's highest-charting hit at the time and was certified platinum in the United States, France, Sweden, Canada, and Norway. And it was certified gold in Australia, New Zealand, Netherlands, Germany, and Switzerland.

"Mask Off" could be viewed as the mainstreaming of drug rap. Although Future does not give context about drug use and addiction in the song, the mentioning of the drugs Molly and Percocet on a top-charting hit provided an eye-opening reality about the normalization of drug use.

Years before the release and success of "Mask Off," I asked Jeezy his thoughts on rap songs that promoted the use of drugs beyond marijuana. He believed that the songs stem from deeper issues within the community.

"They might be mad at me for saying this, but I just think that they might be trying to escape the world they're put in," Jeezy said. "That's what people do to maintain because it's so crazy out here. Nobody is trying to help them or do anything for them, so they have to figure it out on their own. And sometimes that comes with a lot of pain. You got to be a different type of individual to endure that type of pain and that type of suffering and do it sober. That's why your uncle used to drink all the time; he had problems. So, it's like they just run to what they know and that numbs them for the moment. That gets them by. That's their hope and you can't knock that. I get it. People have done it for years and now it's not just the younger generation. You have old white women using prescription drugs all of the time. I don't even like to take aspirin, but that's just me. I'm not here to knock anybody, but that's not my focus."

Along with pill-popping, Lean (Sprite mixed with the drugs Codeine or Promethazine) became another drug heavily promoted in rap songs.

"Codeine is normally used when a person has congestion with a bad cough, and promethazine is anti-nausea medicine that helps with allergy symptoms," Basil Abdur-Rahman, an Atlanta-based pharmacist told me.

"But most people who abuse the drugs are taking ten to fifteen times the normal dose. The common side effects are constipation, blurry vision, hallucination, weight gain, slow heart rate, depression, and it can make it difficult for you to urinate. The thing about narcotics is that once you begin taking them, you develop a tolerance, so you're likely going to want to increase your high. And while you're increasing your high, you do damage to your body that can have long-term effects or lead to death."

UGK's Pimp C died in 2007 from a reported overdose of cough syrup and a pre-existing sleep condition. He was thirty-three years old. Houston's Big Moe also died of a heart attack at the same age. DJ Screw, the founder of the Screwed Up Click and sound, died at twenty-nine of a reported drug overdose.

During the weeks following his death on December 4, 2007, I spoke with Pimp C's partner Bun B about drug abuse in hip-hop.

"It was never anyone's intention to get people to try [Lean]," Bun B admitted. "Syrup was a localized thing that a lot of people didn't know about unless they lived in Texas, Philly, or Oakland, California. There are people in those cities that sip drank, and they don't listen to rap. At the same time, it's a drug that has very serious effects, and a lot of people who are using it are unaware of what it is doing to them. But for anyone sipping syrup, they might want to take a long look at themselves."

Drug abuse in rap reveals a more profound issue when it comes to mental health within the black community. Blacks are more likely to suffer from post-traumatic stress disorder than any other ethnic group in

America, according to a study by the U.S. National Institution of Health. Racism, community violence, and economic restraints can play a part in adding to PTSD in the black community. Unfortunately, blacks are less likely to seek counseling.

Shanti Das, an Atlanta native who played a pivotal role in the careers of OutKast, Goodie Mob, and T.I. during her days as a music executive at LaFace Records and Motown, created a foundation to address mental health disparities in the black community known as Silence the Shame. The organization works to remove the stigma and provide underserved communities with more access to mental health professionals.

"What I see on some music videos and hear in some of the lyrics are artists using recreational drugs as coping mechanisms," Das told me during an interview. "If you're depressed or you have anxiety, you get high to kind of hide it. I'm glad that some of the artists are talking about their own depression and their own struggles, but one of the worse things you can do is to get high or get drunk to mask the problems that you're having. Because that's only going to exacerbate the problem."

Trap History

CHAPTER XI

TRAPPED BY CIRCUMSTANCE: RAP'S DEATH TRAP

Mario Hamilton towered over most but spoke softly. The wiry-framed six-foot-five native of Clayton County, Georgia often held the appearance of a top basketball recruit more so than a rap artist. But after his childhood friend Waka Flocka urged him to step behind the mic, Hamilton became Slim Dunkin and soon found himself signed to Gucci Mane's Brick Squad Monopoly. Dunkin's quiet demeanor turned aggressive when rapping, coinciding perfectly with Waka Flocka's mosh pit style of Trap music on their acclaimed mixtape *Twin Towers*. Stardom was close. Dunkin could almost touch the fame that most young artists coveted.

On December 16, 2011, Dunkin, twenty-five, was reportedly shot and killed by rapper Young Vito during a video shoot at Gucci Mane's Brick Squad studio. The two allegedly argued before their disagreement turned violent. Vito, Vinson Hardimon, was acquitted of murder but convicted of aggravated assault with a deadly weapon. Vito was sentenced to twenty-five years in prison.

Dunkin's story would become an unfortunate theme within Atlanta's Trap music scene. Young rappers who were close to breaking into the mainstream would fall victim to the violence that many of them were hoping to escape by delving into music. They all have stories of gaining success locally, garnering respect from prominent rappers, and being one song or album away from changing their fortunes in life.

Glenn Thomas was more than ready to embrace the spotlight. Raised in Montgomery, Alabama, Thomas viewed Atlanta as a land of promise, a place where the young could create music and gain national attention, at times, overnight. Although Atlanta is only about two hours away from Montgomery, Atlanta seemed like a different planet when Thomas compared it to the rustic lifestyle of his hometown. But the streets and people of Montgomery are what gave rise to Thomas' rap persona, Doe B, a lyricist with a slow flow who shared the mannerisms of The Notorious B.I.G. Doe B possessed the skills and talent to bring attention to Alabama's rap scene, but he needed someone who was already connected to listen.

In 2012, Doe B and his manager, DJ Frank White, drove to Phipps Plaza in Atlanta and scored a meeting with T.I. Doe B would sign to T.I.'s Grand Hustle label and proved his worth on their 2013 compilation album, *Get Dough Or Die*. His songs "Let Me Find Out" and "Kemosabe" became regional hits and prompted Interscope Records to give him a distribution deal for his debut album. 2014 was to be the year that Doe B would realize his dream. But three days before the new year, everything changed.

Gil Scott-Heron once wrote about the paradox of home on the song "Home Is Where the Hatred Is." Contrary to the belief of home being a place of love and comfort, Scott-Heron's home was a place of hopelessness and despair. By the song's end, Scott-Heron comes to the sobering realization that home may be a place to avoid and keep in his past. Unfortunately, the song "Home Is Where the Hatred Is" would reflect Doe B's reality.

Doe B knew that a few people in his hometown would be jealous of his achievements in music, but he never ran from the place he knew best. To celebrate his accomplishments of 2013 and the major projects he had planned for 2014, Doe B returned to his hometown of Montgomery to party with friends and family at Centennial Bar and Grill.

On the night of December 28, 2013, Doe B entered Centennial Bar and Grill and was greeted by most of the patrons as if he was the mayor of the city. He embraced the love but was unprepared for the hate. Old disputes would turn deadly. Darius Thomas, Jason McWilliams, and Taboris Mock reportedly began shooting when some threw a bottle in their direction. Six people were shot and three were killed. Doe B was one of the three who died. Thomas, McWilliams, and Mock were all charged in connection with the murders. Thomas was sentenced to eighty-five years in prison as McWilliams and Mock both pleaded guilty to three counts of assault and were sentenced to 15 years in prison for the charges.

I drove from Atlanta to Montgomery with a colleague to attend Doe B's funeral, which took place on January 4, 2014. Family members dressed in all white as his close friends wore "Rest in Peace" t-shirts with his picture on the front. The entire Grand Hustle team showed their respect as T.I. shared his thoughts on Doe B while speaking at True Divine Baptist Church.

"He carried himself as if he had people to answer to so he couldn't present himself as anything less than," T.I. said while giving Doe B's eulogy. "I saw that day one. At Hustle Gang, I tell every artist that talent will only take them so far. It's what you can do outside of the music that will separate you from the rest. Doe B never left the studio. He said he would rather be in the studio than the club because he knew it would pay off. One thing I will never do is let this man's hard work go to waste. We will make sure his dream lives on."

Similar to Doe B, Trentavious White was close to having it all. Known first as Yung Fresh, Bankroll Fresh recorded songs with Gucci Mane before joining 2 Chainz' Street Execs team. He scored a regional hit in 2014 by paying homage to Cash Money Records' Hot Boys with the single "Hot Boy." The song brought nostalgia to the Cash Money Records era of the early 2000s and inspired Lil Wayne, Juvenile, and Turk to reunite for the remix. Bankroll Fresh followed with the critically-acclaimed mixtapes *Life of a Hot Boy*, part 1 and 2. *Life of a Hot Boy 2* is considered by many as one of the best projects to ever be released in the Trap music genre. Building on his mixtape success, Bankroll Fresh released a short film in 2016, *Take Over Your Trap*, which co-starred 2 Chainz and Skooly.

An alleged disagreement between Bankroll Fresh and rapper No Plug would lead to fatality. On March 5, 2016, Bankroll Fresh and No Plug were both at Street Execs Studios when an altercation occurred between the two over a beef that reportedly began in their neighborhood. At some point, guns were drawn and Bankroll Fresh was shot and killed outside of the studio. Police found fifty shell casings at the scene. No Plug would claim self-defense and was not charged in the crime.

On March 12, 2016, I was present at Jackson Memorial Baptist Church as hundreds of family members and friends paid their respect to Bankroll Fresh and his legacy as an Atlanta rapper. Sister Good Game, who appeared on Jeezy's album *Church in These Streets*, spoke during the ceremony and advised the attendees about making the right decisions in life.

"Black men, you need to put the guns down," Sister Good Game told the audience. "They're handing out more time than you all can imagine. They got the prison designed for you all to fail. I'm going to tell you, young men, you ain't ready to do twenty-five years to life. It's not your decision who lives or die. Don't let [Bankroll] die in vain. He was blessed with two good fathers and a perfect mother. He was raised right. Come on black men, put the guns down! When you get down in the joint, you only got two suits and a lock-up. The same one who told you to pull the trigger, he's gonna leave you. But a change gonna come."

A few days after Bankroll Fresh's homegoing service, I spoke with Big Boi of OutKast. As one of the pioneers who gave Atlanta a voice in rap and popular music, Big Boi spoke out against the violence that touched fellow rappers and the youth.

"It's a shame, he was just starting life," Big Boi said about Bankroll Fresh. "A lot of youngsters these days are desensitized to death because they see it all the time on TV or hear about it. It's nothing to them until they get caught and the consequences behind it. Nobody is with them when the judge gives them basketball numbers and they never get out of jail. You have to think before you act. Rest in peace to Bankroll Fresh, prayers to his family."

There are moments when young artists are on the verge of finding their place in the industry but still confident enough to know that they deserve a spot. They are usually humble and assured about where they belong. They wait patiently for that day, knowing that when their time arrives, they will be more than ready to embrace the light and everything that comes with it. Slim Dunkin, Doe B, and Bankroll Fresh were artists who were poised to gain that success. We knew that they possessed the desire, skill, and right connections to tell their story in a way where millions would pay attention and listen. They should have been the guys who told their stories, traveled the world, matured, and returned to their neighborhoods as shining examples for the next generation, to let youth know that you can come from nothing and become something.

Ermias Asghedom reached that level of maturity through his music and work in the community. Known to the world as Nipsey Hussle, the Los Angeles-based rapper provided examples of how to escape the Trap. Although most of his songs did not classify as Trap music, Nipsey Hussle's life story resonated with every black community in America, including Atlanta.

Nipsey's 2013 *Crenshaw* mixtape was hosted by Atlanta-based DJ Drama. In a move to create a marketing buzz, inspired by the book *Contagious,* Nipsey sold the album for $100 each. Jay-Z would support by buying 100 copies of the project.

In the spring of 2018, I produced an editorial feature with Nipsey Hussle following the release of his Grammy-nominated album, *Victory Lap*. Nipsey spoke about self-empowerment while also focusing on the discipline needed to navigate life and achieve success.

"I got forced into a leadership position before music based on survival," Nipsey Hussle said during an interview at his co-working space Vector 90 in South Central, Los Angeles. "There might be somebody in a leadership position that's making decisions from an uninformed point of view. But the whole unit is going to be affected by this person's decision. So by the laws of survival, whoever had the most informed perspective or the most realistic perspective should lead. We shouldn't let the blind lead the blind. If we're going to do it, let's do this the right way and make it home and not die and not go to jail for life."

On March 31, 2019, Nipsey Hussle was shot and killed in front of The Marathon Clothing store, a location owned by him and his brother, Black Sam. I received a text message about Nipsey Hussle's untimely death while at Los Angeles International Airport on the day of the shooting. Initially scheduled for a return trip to Atlanta, I canceled my flight and drove to the Crenshaw community where hundreds of people gathered at the location where Nipsey lost his life to pay homage to the fallen rapper and businessman.

Tears rolled down the faces of women, children, and even some men. The Crips tied blue bandanas on a fence and lit candles at a makeshift memorial. And the

Nation of Islam kept the community at ease by helping to maintain the peace as emotions ran high. On Crenshaw, nearly every car blasted music by Nipsey Hussle, playing songs such as "Dedication," "Hustle and Motivate," and "Double Up."

One week later, I attended Nipsey Hussle's homegoing service which took place at the Staples Center in Los Angeles. Thousands packed the arena which included notable figures such as Beyoncé, Jay-Z, T.I., The Game, and Kendrick Lamar. Minister Louis Farrakhan and Snoop Dogg eulogized Nipsey. President Barack Obama surprised attendees by issuing a statement on Nipsey's passing that was read by Karen Civil. Stevie Wonder performed Nipsey's favorite song, "Rocket Love," and "Tears in Heaven." Nipsey's mother, father, brother, sister, and girlfriend, Lauren London, all told gut-wrenching stories of how he impacted their lives.

Hours after the homegoing service, the city of Los Angeles stood still for its fallen son. For twenty-five miles, Nipsey's procession made its way through multiple communities, and thousands lined the streets to pay homage one last time. Fans chanted "Nipsey, Nipsey" as his hearse made its way past The Marathon Clothing store. It was the victory lap for a man who became a well-known figure through music, but who inspired many more through his work in the community as a business owner and advocate for teaching inner-city students the importance of science, technology, engineering, and mathematics. If there was a way out of any Trap created by societal circumstances, Nipsey's hustle provided a blueprint to success.

GENTRIFYING THE TRAP

Future reclined while sitting in the backseat of an all-black Sprinter. He clutched two Styrofoam cups, one cup placed inside of the other, and occasionally sipped as his road manager drove into the entrance of the Goat Farm Arts Center. Nestled just west of downtown Atlanta, the center has a rustic feel that's reminiscent of an abandoned town. The brick walls of a gutted factory, built in the 1900s, stood in the center of a large field of dirt, serving as the perfect backdrop for a photoshoot that would depict the Trap in a post-apocalyptic setting.

The interview and photoshoot took place weeks before Future would release his debut album, *Pluto*, in April 2012. At the time, Future garnered a respectable buzz with songs such as "Tony Montana," "Same Damn Time," and "Magic." But he was still working to earn a permanent position in Atlanta's burgeoning Trap music scene.

By 2012, Atlanta's rap scene produced a slew of one-hit wonders who could grab the attention of listeners in the summer and become obscure by the fall of the same year. New rappers needed more than the song of the summer to challenge as possible heirs to Trap music luminaries T.I., Jeezy, and Gucci Mane. To compete with the established rap stars of Atlanta, new artists needed a story.

Future stepped out of the vehicle and continued to hold the Styrofoam cups while walking through the Goat Farm. We found two seats just outside of the gutted brick factory, and he shared details of his youth.

Future's past consisted of his father leaving the household when he was ten-years-old and him occasionally staying with relatives. A few of those relatives served time in prison and succumbed to drug abuse and the drug trade. Those same family members often served as Future's guardians when his mother worked late-night shifts as a 911 operator. At a young age, Future was exposed to some of the darkest realities of life in the Trap.

"When I was coming up, dudes were hanging out everywhere, and you would see junkies just living their everyday life," Future told me during our conversation. "When you live in that type of drug-infested environment, you don't think about being from the streets. It's just your regular life. But when you leave and come back, it's real street shit and it's all in your face."

Future grew up in the Kirkwood neighborhood located east of Atlanta. The drug trade thrived in Kirkwood during the 1980s and 1990s. It bordered East Lake, which was once home to the notorious housing projects East Lake Meadows (known as Lil' Vietnam due to the violence and poor conditions in the complex). It was the place that inspired Future's perception of the Trap and the music that would follow.

But the legacy of Kirkwood extends beyond the Trap. Kirkwood remains prominent in the history of black Atlanta. When the Chicago-based Pullman Company opened a rail repair station in Kirkwood during the 1920s, the firm became one of the largest employers of blacks in America at the time. But while blacks were able to find employment at Pullman, Kirkwood schools remained segregated until 1965. And once the schools were desegregated by law, white flight occurred and it became a majority-black community.

But the Kirkwood that Future knew during his youth was much different from what it has become. Once a majority black neighborhood, gentrification in the mid-2000s caused the community to become a much smaller version of Brooklyn, New York. Wealthier white residents moved in and, subsequently, the property taxes increased annually. Within ten years, median home sale prices increased by 275 percent, and property taxes increased by forty percent. Many of the black homeowners who lived in Kirkwood for decades were unable to pay the rising property taxes and were eventually displaced.

In 1990, white residents only represented one percent of the Kirkwood community. That year, a home in Kirkwood could be purchased for as low as $60,000. By 2017, houses in Kirkwood were priced as high as $1 million and the black population had fallen below fifty percent. In July of 2017, Georgia Building Authority sold the abandoned building and property that once served as headquarters for the Pullman Company to the California-based production company Atomic Entertainment for $8 million. Atomic Entertainment decided to build a film complex and condos at the location.

Kirkwood serves as a microcosm of the reverse white

flight that continues to take place in Atlanta and other predominantly black cities nationwide. In the 1960s, white residents in Atlanta complained to city officials and even put up physical barriers to keep blacks out of certain areas. When a Morehouse College graduate, Dr. Clinton Warner, purchased a home in the all-white Peyton Forest community in 1962, white residents complained to Mayor Ivan Allen about the potential of more blacks moving into the community.

In an attempt to appease white residents and prevent further "intrusion" by black residents, Mayor Allen signed legislation that ordered the building of barricades around Peyton Forest. Civil rights leaders and protesters marched on City Hall and called the barriers Atlanta's version of Germany's Berlin Wall. A judge would eventually rule the barricades to be unconstitutional, and they were removed three months later. White families vacated Peyton Forest and other locations within the city of Atlanta in droves during the 1960s. Forty years later, a multitude of white residents returned to the city. But instead of barricades, high real estate prices fueled a form of new-age segregation.

In the fall of 1999, a Georgia Tech graduate student imagined a system that could bring Atlanta's neighborhoods together while possibly easing the city's horrific traffic issues. Ryan Gravel's master thesis focused on the idea of a loop that connected various communities in Atlanta by trial and transit. Gravel's plan would allow Atlantans to break their dependency on cars being their primary means of transportation. The project became known as the BeltLine.

The BeltLine would consist of walking and bike trails, shops, street art, a skate park, and newly constructed condos and apartments. Some of the forty-five neighborhoods that would be connected by the path included predominantly black communities such as West End, Old Fourth Ward, Adair Park, Mechanicsville, Sylvan Hills, Oakland City, Washington Park, and Pittsburgh to name a few. In theory, the creation of the twenty-two-mile BeltLine would improve the standard of life in Atlanta. However, it soon became a project that many feared would gut the livelihood and culture of most of Atlanta's black communities.

From day one of the initial planning, which began in 2003, controversy followed the BeltLine. The Atlanta City Council signed a law that required a portion of new development on the BeltLine to be set aside for low-income and subsidized housing. Atlanta BeltLine Inc. thus agreed to build 5,600 affordable homes. By 2017, only 785 affordable housing units were built, and two hundred of those homes were still under construction. Home prices near or on the BeltLine soared by sixty percent from 2012 to 2015 versus a thirty percent increase in other sections of Atlanta. The median prices for condos and apartments on the north end, southwest end, and east end of the BeltLine increased to $250,000 and over, or over fifty percent of the average median home price in Atlanta. Some condos reached prices that were $400,000 and above.

Traditional black communities were compromised in the name of growth. This mishap occurred in a city where black mayors and a majority-black city council were trusted to provide leadership and protect the most vulnerable. Political leaders turned their backs on the people who drove the culture of Atlanta only to appease real estate investors and developers who could gain wealth from the city's land while ignoring the displacement of thousands.

Matt Bronfman, CEO of Jamestown, the company that developed Ponce City Market in Atlanta's Old Fourth Ward, attempted to defend gentrification to the public by presenting a myopic view of its effects on a city. On June 22, 2017, Bronfman endorsed gentrification as a necessary factor for the growth of a city during a town hall for the American Jewish Committee's ACCESS in the ATL.

Bronfman's statement was that of a person who appeared to lack empathy for the people who are affected the most by gentrification. Gentrification is necessary for Bronfman because his company will thrive from the benefits. But gentrification often begins with the displacement of black residents and leads to a disconnect between the new residents and the old residents who remain.

To control the ensuing damage, several grassroots organizations and city officials proposed plans that would assist residents in highly gentrified areas. Mayor Kasim Reed served as head of the nonprofit Westside Future Fund. The organization's main priority was to create affordable housing in black communities on the west side of the city such as English Avenue, Vine City, Washington Park, Ashview Heights, and the AUC.

The organization also introduced the Anti-Displacement Tax Fund in the spring of 2017. The goal of the fund was to raise $5 million from the private sector to help homeowners pay the increases in taxes.

The Westside Future Fund is an initiative that can help curb the displacement caused by gentrification. However, there is a battle for Atlanta. And some of the people who are looking to claim the city are against any form of inclusion. They are fueled by hate and are seeking to make Atlanta a city that represents the essence of the old South.

When I interviewed T.I. in 2017, he talked about the reality of gentrification in Atlanta. For him, and many others in the city, it's vital that the culture of Atlanta remains secure even if the black population loses its strength in numbers.

"There are some conservative 'stuffies' who want to take [the city] over," T.I. said. "They just want to tear down everything and build big buildings. But Atlanta isn't about that. It's not about black and white to me. It's about culture. Even if Atlanta is no longer a majority-black city, it's important that the culture remains rich. For instance, Harlem has been gentrified, but the Apollo is still the Apollo. When the Apollo isn't the Apollo anymore, Harlem will no longer be Harlem. You have to change in order to grow. But as long as it doesn't lose its identity in that growth, we can still win. I know some cool white people who have good vibes and have great perspectives. But you're not about to bring that Tiki torch white shit to Atlanta. It's not just about my generation; it's about the people who came before us, such as Andrew Young, Dr. Martin Luther King, and Joseph E. Lowery. We aren't going to let their legacy go out bad."

Trap History

PART III: BEYOND THE TRAP

CHAPTER XIII

TRAP MONUMENTS

The Pink Trap House

Moments before sunset, west of downtown Atlanta in the middle of summer in 2017, the Pink Trap House was being painted white. The white paint represented the impending end of 2 Chainz's brainchild that existed for several weeks as a physical representation to his fourth album, *Pretty Girls Like Trap Music*.

2 Chainz leased the house on Howell Mill Road and painted it bright pink with the word "Trap" painted in black on the tympanum of the house. A pink stove with pots sat in the front yard next to an old pink car. Inside, the Pink Trap House featured artwork and offered painting classes, free HIV testing, and church services on specific dates. Overall, it proved to be a good marketing idea by 2 Chainz, who was able to bring the concept of his album to life.

"It was a part of the activation I was doing when I was coming up with concepts for the album, *Pretty Girls Like Trap Music*," 2 Chainz shared with me. "I came up with Pink Trap House because I associated pink with being pretty. I had a bunch of ideas which included everything from a pink stove to a pink Chevy. And it was just about making things that people saw as eyesores, beautiful. We got tremendous feedback and we still get good feedback from it. You know, every other day somebody mentions the Pink Trap House and I appreciate it. We had everything from an HIV clinic, to church. We did a lot of good things."

Born and raised in College Park, Georgia, 2 Chainz initially entered the rap game with the name Tity Boi and as a member of the duo Playaz Circle. Along with his childhood friend Dolla Boy, the group would sign to Ludacris' Disturbing Tha Peace record label with distribution by Def Jam. Playaz Circle would score their biggest hit with an assist from Lil Wayne on the 2007 song "Duffle Bag Boys." But after the release of their sophomore album, *Flight 360: The Takeoff*, Tity Boi would go solo, rebrand himself as 2 Chainz, and release the classic mixtape *Codeine Cowboys*. He would eventually sign a solo deal with Def Jam and released his critically-acclaimed solo debut, *Based on a T.R.U. Story*, in 2012. By 2017, 2 Chainz stood as one of the top stars in rap. The album *Pretty Girls Like Trap Music* would take his brand to a new level.

The Pink Trap House eventually became a landmark mostly due to its presence on social media. People of all ages and racial and socioeconomic backgrounds took photos and captured videos in front of the house and posted the images on their Instagram, Snapchat, Facebook, and Twitter accounts. Some drove for hours from other cities and a few people flew into Atlanta just to see the house. I encountered two women from Amsterdam who decided to visit the Pink Trap House because of their love for Trap music. The women followed the music of 2 Chainz, Gucci Mane, and Migos by watching videos on YouTube and listening to SoundCloud. The Pink Trap House made their love for Trap music tangible by turning the Trap into an interactive experience. However, the Pink Trap House was painted white and closed following the end of 2 Chainz's album promotion. One year later, another Atlanta artist would create a museum dedicated to the city's rising music scene.

TRAP MUSIC MUSEUM

Inside of a warehouse on the Westside of Atlanta, the Trap came to life. But unlike the drug Traps that were common in impoverished areas of the city of Atlanta, this Trap turned pain into art. T.I. decided to highlight the culture of Trap music with the Trap Music Museum.

"I want to thank people who made this their life's passion for the past nine months," T.I. said about the museum during its opening night in September 2018. "One person cannot fulfill the prophecy of a masterpiece. Us being able to put our minds together and share our thoughts, it all continued to what you see today. We share in this together."

The exhibit consisted of multiple art installations such as T.I.'s safe room which featured a slew of automatic weapons, clothing, and a Grammy Award. Gucci Mane's Trap kitchen included a table with baking soda, artificial drugs and paraphernalia, fake money, and a makeshift stove. Jeezy's snow room featured all-white kilos of cocaine made of styrofoam and snowman which coincided with the rapper's "Snowman" theme. Other rappers such as Migos, 21 Savage, Rick Ross, Future, 2 Chainz, and YFN Lucci and more were all featured in various works of art. The art was compiled and curated by Antwanette McLaughlin, Marina Skye Williams, Lalanya Abner, and Atlanta artist Maiya Bailey.

"I initially got a call from T.I.'s team about the idea of a Trap house called 'Escape the Trap,'" McLaughlin told me during an interview days before it was set to open to the public. "We redeveloped the idea and decided to make it an experience where they can see trap art and make their way to an escape room. We wanted people to be able to walk away with an experience."

Maiya Bailey shared how the museum is connecting Atlanta's art and rap worlds. "The art scene and music scene [are] often alienated from each other in Atlanta," Bailey said. "The Trap Museum is bringing both worlds together."

For nearly nine months, a team worked to construct the exhibit in a building owned by T.I. "Seeing the transformation of this process was the best part," Williams said. "Being able to see this come to life is amazing. It's a groundbreaking situation. Having been a part of this movement is special. It's interesting that people learn the history around the subculture."

But beyond the art, it was important for the imagery also to reflect the truth about the neglect that occurs in the black community.

"You can glamorize this, but we also have a R.I.P. section that's heartbreaking," Abner told me during an interview before the grand opening. "A lot of it ends in death or incarceration. So the biggest thing is that [T.I.] escaped the trap. That's why we have that feature. This culture was built from pain, but we took the pain and [made] it art."

21 SAVAGE'S MOTEL 21

Outside of Motel 21, an aura of danger loomed. The building stood next to a wooded area in a blighted section of Glenwood Road in East Atlanta. A vacant bar directly across the street served as a second parking lot for visitors. On the night I visited, a few men and women, who appeared to be drifters, wandered around the dimly lit area, braving the cold night air in mid-December. At a nearby liquor store, several men congregated outside. Indeed, this was the heart of East Atlanta, Zone 6, a place where poverty entraps, and the possibilities of dreams are often swallowed whole.

Shortly after 7 p.m. on the night of Dec. 20, 2018, hundreds of people stood in the cold and rain and lined up outside of Motel 21 to get a glimpse of the art exhibit and hear one of the most anticipated albums of the year, 21 Savage's *I Am > I Was*.

Motel 21 was another creation by Antwanette McLaughlin and Marina Skye Williams, two of the curators of T.I.'s Trap Music Museum. The motel was once known as the Glen Royal Inn, a place where crime and violence were more common than it serving as a place where individuals and families could find rest for the night.

"Y'all never saw an album release party in the hood," 21 Savage told me after previewing his album. "I'm the first rapper to have a listening party at a crack motel. This is a crack head motel where there was a lot of prostitution and murder."

At Motel 21, the two-story structure was illuminated by red lights with the words "No Vacancy" painted across the building. Before walking inside, several armed guards checked visitors thoroughly, searching for weapons, ensuring that violence would only be present through the lyrics and art.

Once inside, the allure of sex, drugs, money, and violence were plentiful, in an artistic way. In all, there were eleven rooms, and each room served as a visual representation of songs from 21 Savage's Grammy Award-nominated album, *I Am > I Was*.

TRAPLOITATION VS. TRAP EXPLORATION

Trap monuments and art exhibits provided a glimpse of the Trap for tourists. But there will always be a thin line between exploration and exploitation. While hundreds of people smiled and rejoiced while taking pictures in front of the art installations, it may never provide the true feeling of being in a real Trap house. If some of the attendees were forced to visit a real Trap house in the Bluff or East Atlanta, most of the smiles would have been replaced with looks of shock, fear, and awe.

There is nothing fun, funny, or Instagram-worthy about the Trap houses that serve as reminders of the captivity produced by drug addiction and poverty. But the same pain that was created by drugs and poverty also inspired Trap music. To ignore its impact is to ignore reality and culture.

The city of Atlanta and the state of Georgia has not always embraced its greatest entertainment asset, black music. Every major city in America has a rap scene, but every rap scene does not have a national or global presence. Since OutKast released its debut album in 1994, over 100 Atlanta-based rappers and producers have gained prominence in the music industry.

It took a while for city officials in Atlanta to promote its victories in terms of music. There were not any landmarks, bars, or museums that highlighted Atlanta's importance to music culture. Atlanta did not feel like a town that was home to some of the greatest rappers and producers in the world.

In contrast, Nashville, Tennessee embraced country music for decades. Fans of country music can visit Nashville and experience the Country Music Hall of Fame and Museum, Grand Ole Opry, Johnny Cash Museum, and Historic Printers Alley.

On December 23, 2017, Atlanta Mayor Keisha Lance Bottoms announced the Creative Industries Loan Fund. The initiative offered loans of up to $100,000 for local creative entrepreneurs to use for their creative projects.

It was a step forward to empower the creatives who helped to bring attention to the city of Atlanta.

So while some may view Trap monuments as a form of exploitation, Trap music is a part of Atlanta's history. The Pink Trap House, Trap Music Museum, and Motel 21 proved that people from different races, regions, socio-economic backgrounds and countries would travel for miles and spend money in the city to experience and learn more about Atlanta's music culture.

TRAPPIN' AROUND THE WORLD

Berlin, Germany is nearly five thousand miles away from Atlanta, but it's a place where you could find Trap music. On any given night during the weekend, hundreds would stand in line with the hopes of experiencing a new high. They were anticipating entry into one of the most celebrated clubs in Europe.

Club GRETCHEN was not just a nightspot where parties ended well after sunrise. It was a place where some of the top Trap DJs in Europe presented their craft. But the patrons did not encounter the sounds of DJ Toomp, Shawty Redd, Mike Will Made-It, Metro Boomin, 808 Mafia, or any other Atlanta-based DJs or producers of Trap music. In Europe, EDM Trap rules.

EDM Trap (Electronic Dance Music) is an offshoot of techno, and dubstep, genres that were all inspired by house music, a genre of music created by Black musicians in Chicago. The major similarity EDM Trap has with Atlanta's version of Trap is the use of vocal chops and the TR-808 beat machine which serves as the essential component of Trap EDM. Otherwise, Trap music and EDM Trap are different genres that share a common name.

Coincidentally, EDM Trap received its moniker by

accident. The origins of EDM Trap can be traced to Josh "J2K" Young and Curt "Autobot" Cameruci. In the mid-2000s, J2K and Autobot were Chicago-based DJs/producers searching for ways to build their brand while performing sets across the nation.

With their DJ sets failing to build significant buzz, Autobot, a producer since his teenage years, decided to teach J2K the intricacies of music production. The duo soon began collaborating on tracks and sending their music to artists with the hopes of getting a placement on an album or mixtape. However, artists would hold the songs for months without adding vocals to the instrumentals.

J2K and Autobot decided to give their music away for free by uploading the instrumentals to SoundCloud.

One particular instrumental combined the synths of techno and rave music found in European clubs with the snares and drum kicks of Atlanta-based Trap music. J2K intended for the track to be used by a rapper. When uploading the instrumental to SoundCloud, he wrote "Trap" as the genre. The song, "Total Recall," became an online sensation and led to the release of an EP which featured instrumentals produced by J2K and Autobot, now known as Flosstradamus.

Many of the fans who gravitated to "Total Recall" were oblivious to Southern-based Trap music and began calling Flosstradamus' sound "Trap" in regards to the original SoundCloud post.

By the end of 2012, Flosstradamus was selling out arenas, and other DJs such as Baauer ("Harlem Shake"), UZ ("Trap Shit 6/9"), and RL Grime ("Mercy" remix) emerged on the scene. Hundreds of bedroom producers uploaded their versions of EDM Trap to SoundCloud, and the subgenre soon became a worldwide phenomenon.

"Once I started to play at venues in Berlin, people were going crazy to EDM Trap," DJ Gün who hails from the Berlin, German, told me during an interview. "Many people over here enjoy house, techno, electronic music, and dubstep. This new type of Trap music combines a lot of these genres and that's why it became so popular over here. But when it comes to hip-hop's version of Trap, it's different because both genres have different meanings or origins. There is a different story behind it. EDM Trap is really all about the bass, not much about the lyrics."

For some, the biggest issue with EDM Trap is that it borrows the 808 drums and snares of traditional Trap music without presenting the full story. Because EDM Trap is mostly predicated on a sound, it lacks the context provided by rappers who are describing their environment. The instrumentals of Trap music can be co-opted, but the narrative represents issues that run deeper than screwed-up voiceovers and a bass drop.

"When I first heard EDM Trap, people were telling me that it was taking Trap music to another level," legendary Atlanta producer DJ Toomp explained. "But there is nobody rapping, so how is that Trap music? When the young generation comes up with something new, they should name it something that reflects what it is. Don't confuse people and call it something else. Maybe we should have trademarked the name to make sure that no confusion is out here twenty years from now. When you come up with something, don't get so caught up into what's done in the past. Try to make some new stuff, but also give it a new title."

Jeezy shared similar thoughts about Trap music and EDM. "When I started working with [producer] Shawty Redd, I would put the snare on the two instead of the one in order to slow the music down," Jeezy said about the process of producing songs such as "Get Ya Mind Right." "Then the beat would build and I wanted the bass to drop at a certain point. I wanted people to listen [to what I was saying] instead of just dancing. When I hear EDM I just laugh because I wonder if they know that we actually sat in a basement and really thought about that shit. We made changes [to the beat] so that it would be slower and gothic. The sounds were darker and had more texture to it."

There are good and bad consequences of the Trap sound that originated in Atlanta being co-opted by producers from other countries and music genres.

"I get irritated by it sometimes because it's like a lot of people are not being original," Zaytoven expressed to me. "The music has got to the point where all people are doing is copying what somebody else is doing. But there are pros and cons to it. It's almost overwhelming because when I started doing music, I never thought it would be such a big influence on different kinds of music. [Trap] influences almost every genre of music right now."

GLOBAL TRAPPIN'

Elements of Trap music can be found in every continent around the world.

Mthembeni "Emtee" Ndevuo developed a love for music early in life while growing up in Matatiele, a small village in Eastern Cape, South Africa. Emtee first performed in front of a crowd at 9-years-old at a school talent show and later became the youngest choir conductor at the renown Barnato Park High School in Johannesburg. But during his teenage years, Emtee would also discover Trap music through websites and at parties in South Africa.

"I first started to like Trap [music] by listening to Gucci Mane, T.I., and Jeezy," Emtee told me during an interview in 2019. "Atlanta's influence is significant. They play a lot of Atlanta Trap [music] in [South African] nightclubs. Atlanta is on right now. The music is more meaningful for people like me."

In 2015, Emtee and his producer Ruff began to craft their own version of Trap music with the release of the song "Roll Up." The production and overall sound of "Roll Up" is similar to Wiz Khalifa's "We Dem Boyz." However, Emtee added his own flavor to "Roll Up" by rapping in English and the indigenous Zulu language, IsiZulu. The song opened the door for his 2015 platinum-selling debut album *Avery*, an album that is considered by many to be Africa's first significant Trap music album.

"It came from a love of hip-hop," Emtee told me about creating an entire album based off of the sounds and styles of traditional Trap music. "I believed that I could do it on my own. Trap is similar to my lifestyle. Coming from the hood. We're all going through the same things. It's stories about where we come from."

Emtee would lead a movement known as ATM

(African Trap Music) which featured other South African Trap music artists such Nasty C who released the hit "Hell Naw" and Sjava who won a BET Award in 2018 for Viewers' Choice Best International Act. They provided an inside look at South Africa's Trap music movement with the documentary series, *ATM*.

France is another country with a significant Trap music scene. In France, Guy2Bezbar rapped with the same aggression as Waka Flocka on his hit songs "Ah Non C'est Terrible" and "Lady Melodie." Rapper Gradur also used highly-charged vocals over Trap beats for his songs "La Peuf" and "On est Pas Tout Seul." Boiler Room TV once called Gradur, "France's greatest straight-up Trap ambassador." But rapper MHD is arguably the most influential Trap music artist to emerge from France. While combining traditional Trap music with West African music, MHD's "Afro Trap Part. 1" amassed nearly twenty-five million views on YouTube within two years of its release in 2015. His 2016 video "Afro Trap Part. 7" garnered over 183 million views on YouTube in two years.

In China, the Higher Brothers became known as the Chinese version of Migos following the release of "Made in China" and "Franklin." The record label that signed the group, 88rising, led the way in highlighting Trap music in Asia with their artists Rich Brian and Keith Ape who hails from Korea. Keith Ape's "It G Ma," garnered over 65 million views on YouTube in four years. A remix featuring Waka Flocka Flame and A$AP Ferg made the song more palatable for American listeners.

Latin Trap music reached the mainstream faster

than any other form of international Trap music. Latin artists such as Bad Bunny, Ozuna, and J Balvin found ways to give their version of Trap music a more pop sound that led to chart-topping hits such as Bad Bunny's "I Like It," which featured Cardi B.

In Mexico, a genre known as Trap-Corrido features artists who provide a perspective of Mexico's vast drug war with themes of violence, crime, and life inside of a drug cartel. Prominent Trap-Corrido artists include Alemán, La Plebada, Fntxy, and Cozy Cuz.

Morocco also created an emerging Trap music scene with the "post-cultural" collective known as NAAR. Established by Mohammed Sqalli and Ilyes Griyeb, NAAR produced and promoted Moroccan Trap music artists such as Shayfeen and Issam.

The instrumentation and vocal cadence used by the artists and producers of Trap music could be the key to its international influence. Artists from around the world gravitated to the sounds created on the streets of Bankhead, Campbellton Road, and East Atlanta.

"You can do anything with it," Emtee shared with me when discussing Trap music's global appeal. "You can talk about different things with the music. What I discovered was that you can have a lot of fun making it. It comes from an environment. It will be more people who will want to be a part of the music [in the future]. The proof of the success is there."

Trap History

**TRAP - AMERICAN MUSIC.
AMERICAN PROBLEM.
AMERICAN DREAM.**

Art is often used as a coping mechanism and a tool to make sense out of painful situations. When presented honestly and void of exploitation, Trap music can capture the hurt, sorrow, and desperation of searching for a way out when there appears to be none. The pain expressed through Trap music is similar to the personal agony experienced by blues artists. If there were ever a genre of music that closely relates to Trap music, it would be the blues. Both genres of music were created out of grim conditions and disadvantages that stem from racism.

The blues found its origins in the field songs and spirituals sung during slavery. Shaped by the human injustice of slavery and the Jim Crow era of the South, the blues tugged at the raw emotions of the black experience. The music revealed the complexities of black America's condition which was created by discrimination, economic inequality, and inadequate education during the 20th century.

Fast forward to the 21st century and blacks continued to face some of the same societal issues that hindered previous generations. By the year 2000, blacks had made tremendous strides in nearly every facet of life in America, but there were still severe problems that affected the entire black community. The blues and Trap music are both art forms inspired by black plight.

"When you [think of] the blues, it's the same thing as Trap[music]," blues legend Bobby Rush shared. "When you're trapped in a situation and there's no place to go. It's the music that's created when your back is up against the wall."

If Future had been born decades earlier, he could have been a blues artist due to his knack for melodic storytelling. Future's voice exudes pain. Dysfunction is revealed through his lyrics and delivery. Naturally raspy, his voice, at times, can be eerie and menacing. His slurred rhymes and wailing conveys the despair of those trapped by poverty, crime, and a lack of guidance.

On songs such as "March Madness," Future sounds as if he's confessing his troubles to a psychiatrist while rapping about police brutality, regrets of infidelity, and taking drugs in an attempt to numb life's pain. Future can emanate the braggadocio of a well-paid dope boy in one verse while also revealing the vulnerability of a depressed person who may embrace substances to escape harsh realities.

You can also hear remnants of the blues in the high-pitched crooning of Young Thug, and the melodic rap flows of Lil Baby and YFN Lucci.

"The links between Trap music and the blues are fairly obvious," blues artist Sammy Blues said. "With Trap, the voice becomes the guitar or other instrument. It's young blacks expressing the need to escape oppression and poverty by whatever means necessary. It's a common theme of coming up in a system that discriminates against young blacks. The difference is that instead of bootleg alcohol and juke joints, it's the club life and cocaine. Muddy Waters sang about 'Champagne & Reefer.' Robert Johnson wrote '32-20' about having a gun in the 1930s. And Howling Wolf sang 'Forty-Four' in the 1950s. Songs like 'That Reefer Man' predate even those songs. Ma Rainy, Bessie Smith, and Ida Cox sang about sex as did Millie Jackson long before Nicki Minaj. The basic subjects and motivations are the same."

AMERICAN PROBLEM

Poverty can be generational. And without clear answers on how to escape poverty, the youth must often figure a way out for themselves.

There are not many ways for kids who come from underprivileged homes and environments to break into mainstream American society without gaining an exceptional education, utilizing a superior talent, or gaining access to a life-changing opportunity.

In most professional sports, teams with losing records have a chance to win the top pick in the draft once the season concludes. It's a system that attempts to level the playing field by offering subpar teams a chance at obtaining the best athletic talent. However, a draft does not exist to help increase the chances for a level playing field when it comes to education and financial success. Kids from impoverished communities are at a severe disadvantage when compared to the kids who reside in more affluent communities. A school voucher or scholarship will not always level the playing field.

It can be argued that most American public schools have not taught poor students how to become wealthy. Instead, public schools have taught poor students how to become better workers for the wealthy.

Most public school systems have not taught kids the value of investing in real estate, the importance of opening a 401K and saving for retirement, or the basics of how to obtain a business loan and start a business.

And while graduating high school and earning a college degree is often presented as the great equalizer, an enormous gap remains when it comes to race and wealth. Blacks who graduate college have a better chance of accumulating more wealth over time than blacks who don't earn a college degree. But black college graduates are still far behind their white counterparts. Black college graduates usually carry twice as much loan debt as white graduates and are more likely to default on their student loans. As a result, a family headed by a black college graduate has less wealth on average than a white family headed by a high school dropout.

"When blacks graduate [college], they are more likely to have a significant level of higher debt, they are less likely to come from families that can help them with the next steps in life," Duke University economist Dr. William Darity, Jr. shared with me. "That's including being able to receive help from family members when it comes to the down payment on a home. They are less likely to come from families that can give them a significant amount of funds to boost them on their way to their adult lives. So if anything, more highly educated blacks may be carrying a substantially greater debt burden as a consequence of obtaining higher education, although the higher education provides them with better employment opportunities than blacks without comparable degrees. But there is a real difference during graduation from the average black student and the average white student in terms of the resources and amounts that they can receive from families or extended families."

The lack of options can lead to young men and women using the Trap as a way to earn a living. It's an occupation where the turnover rates are high, and dealers believe in the small chance of changing their financial future through drug sales. Desperation reigns when survival stands as the only goal.

"These kids that are out here [drug] dealing, they're not stupid," Killer Mike shared with me. "That's why they made the decision to get some money because we told them that making money is more important than education. We don't value education. You don't take your children around college professors and brand them. You take them around athletes and famous people. Children learn early what money means. What we're not doing is showing our children that there's a way to get money that's not fast, not quick. We just kill their confidence so young and that's why they accept Trap life or have dreams of [selling drugs] out of a bando. You have to tell them to do responsible things that's an investment into a real future. That's what the young men who make it out of the Trap do."

Trap music was birthed out of the frustration of being confined while existing as a free citizen in America. In its purest form, Trap music is poverty transformed into art.

There is a sense of hurt, anguish, confusion, and immediacy within the production and lyrics of Trap music. The greatest songs ever written were inspired by heartbreak. Trap music is the sound of heartbreak. It's the heartbreak of seeing kids who realize that their lives will be filled with limitations. It's the heartbreak of being unqualified to land a legitimate job to support yourself and change the circumstances of your family. It's the heartbreak of having to sell sickness to bring home income. And even when Trap music celebrates the indulging of sex, popping pills, and drinking Lean, it's all from wanting to experience some high due to being relegated to living a life that is so low.

"Everybody wants to do better," Jeezy shared. "We all aspire to be the guy who can take care of our neighborhood. So that's why when you say 'Trap,' it's a place where you handle your business, and it can go either way. If you don't make it, you will for sure be trapped because you might end up doing some real-time, or being killed. Those are the things that you go through. It's not something that we're proud of doing. But If I'm not going out harming people at gunpoint and I'm a man out here grinding dollar for dollar and risking my life, I feel like I'm not doing anything wrong. That's all that I see around me. I'm not a taker. I'm an earner. I'd rather earn every dollar I get. And that's why we call it the Trap. We're proud that we're [finally] able to take care of our families."

AMERICAN DREAM

An eight-year-old child named Keisha saw police cars surrounding her family's home after she arrived from school. Once inside, police officers forced her and her siblings to remain on the couch as her father was being taken away in handcuffs. He was arrested and convicted of cocaine distribution. For the next three years, Keisha would only see her father on weekends while visiting him at a Georgia prison.

The young woman, raised on the Westside of Atlanta, would seek to rise above her family's issues by staying focused on education while attending the all-black public school Frederick Douglass High and earning college degrees from FAMU and Georgia State University. On Dec. 5, 2017, Keisha Lance Bottoms beat the odds and became the sixtieth mayor of Atlanta.

During her first few weeks in office, Bottoms made a connection with Atlanta's rap community. She named T.I. and Killer Mike as members of her transition team. It was the first time in the city's history that rappers had received such an honor. In a sense, it was a sign that Atlanta's music culture had come full circle. Artists who gave voice to their plight were now at a powerful political table. Christopher Hicks, a former music industry executive at Def Jam, was named as the new director of the Mayor's Office of Film and Entertainment.

Bottoms understood that the cultural power of Trap music and Atlanta's arts scene must be supported politically. She also knew that the societal aspects of the Trap must be examined to create better-living conditions for the citizens of Atlanta.

"What you see with Trap music, you're seeing a reflection of what people are feeling on the streets and in our communities," Keisha Lance Bottoms told me in an interview one week after she was elected mayor of Atlanta. "I think that it's important that we embrace it because there are lessons to be learned in it and there are things to be gleaned. And also just in terms of how we continue to embrace arts and culture in Atlanta in general. Whether or not there are people who like Trap music or don't like Trap music and don't agree with the messaging, it's a reflection of what people are seeing and feeling each and every day. And I think it's something we have to continue to be cognizant of especially if we really want to know what young people in our communities are feeling."

ATLANTA BURNS

The city of Atlanta burned on the night of May 29, 2020, after the death of George Floyd sparked a revolution. Floyd was killed on May 25, 2020, by a white Minneapolis police officer named Derek Chauvin who kneeled on Floyd's neck for eight minutes and forty-six seconds. A teenage bystander captured Floyd's death with a cell phone video camera and that video eventually went viral.

The anger caused by the ongoing oppression of black people reached a boiling point. Atlantans responded to Floyd's death with a protest march on May 29, 2020, that took place at Centennial Olympic Park in downtown Atlanta. When the darkness of night approached, some set police cars on fire, destroyed property at the CNN Center, College Football Hall of Fame and some protesters also looted stores in the city's affluent Buckhead area.

In an attempt to bring calm to a tense situation, Mayor Keisha Lance Bottoms held a press conference and called on Killer Mike and T.I. to provide a bit of guidance to youth protestors. Killer Mike gave a gut-wrenching speech about race, police brutality, and unrest in America.

"I'm mad as hell," Killer Mike said durig the press conference. "I woke up wanting to see the world burn down yesterday because I'm tired of seeing black men die. He casually put his knee on a human being's neck for nine minutes as he died like a zebra in the clutch of a lion's jaw. And we watch it like murder porn over and over again. So that's why children are burning it to the ground. They don't know what else to do."

Several days later, Atlanta captured the attention of the nation after another black man, Rayshard Brooks, was shot and killed by a white police officer, Garrett Rolfe. Brooks, 27, fell asleep at a Wendy's drive-thru. When authorities arrived, they suspected that Brooks was drunk and gave him a sobriety test that he reportedly failed. During his conversation with police officers, Brooks asked if he could leave his car parked at Wendy's and walk home. A struggle ensued and Brooks was shot in the back while running away. Rolfe was fired from the Atlanta Police Department and charged with first-degree murder.

At a time when Atlanta continued to be front and center in the fight for social justice, Lil Baby would lend his voice to the movement for racial equality. On June 6, 2020, Lil Baby released "The Bigger Picture," a song that perfectly described the angst of black youth fed up by years of racial injustice and police brutality. The production, handled by producer Noah, featured a traditional Trap music beat, but Lil Baby's lyrics were as important to the movement as Curtis Mayfield's "People Get Ready," Marvin Gaye's "What's Going On," Public Enemy's "Fight The Power," and Kendrick Lamar's "Alright."

Atlanta turned the tragedy of the Trap into triumph through music. It's a city where black kids found their voice, told their stories, and inspired the world. An enthusiastic spirit exists in Trap music even in its darkest verses. It's the sound of resistance that revealed how kids from low-income backgrounds found a way out of no way. The music tells a survivor's story backed by the most fierce production in the history of rap.

The word Trap also became a term embraced by corporations and businesses. AT&T sponsored a touring event known as TRAP Karaoke. Across the nation, small businesses have created events centered around Trap music such as Trap Yoga, Trap and Paint, Trap Cycle, and Trap fitness. And there is a slew of T-shirts and clothing companies that use the term Trap on their products.

But the Trap is also drenched in tragedy. The Trap serves as evidence of the ongoing pain and abuse inflicted on black communities for centuries. The next generation must not be subjected to environments that create physical and social barriers. We must get to a point where the Trap can only be viewed through a retrospective lens, a place and mentality that once existed while no longer being a way of life caused by unfortunate circumstances.

Our communities must not lean on addiction as a means to cope with the trauma of the past, the discomfort of the present, or the uncertainty of what's to come.

The history of Trap has been written, but the vision for a new day must be adapted for future generations who should never have to experience the ills of the Trap beyond the music which captures its story.

A.R. Shaw

THANK YOU!

I want to thank my mother, father, sisters, brother, grandmother, aunts, cousins and all family members and friends who provided love, encouragement and support throughout the years. To everyone who helped with this project in any capacity, thank you! Special thanks to Calaya Stallworth, Kareem Kenyada, Joe Moss, Soweto Bosia, Chance Uno, Ronda Racha Penrice, Robert D. Lee, Codicast Studios, Billy Johnson, Peyton Chambers, Brittney Keith, Mare of NEA Records, Louis Cuthbert, Norman Johnson, Justin Dennis, Neima Abdulahi, Maurice Garland, Nick Love, Khujo Goodie, Ms. Ricci, Canton Jones. Thanks to Munson Steed and everyone at Rolling Out for providing me an opportunity to practice the craft of journalism. Respect to all artists and industry talent who shared their stories with me during their career such as OutKast, Organized Noize, T.I., Jeezy, Gucci Mane, Killer Mike, DJ Toomp, DJ Drama, Zaytoven, Sonny Digital, Migos, Young Thug, 2 Chainz, Future, Kawan Prather, Shanti Das and the publicists/managers who helped to facilitate interviews. Thanks to Dr. William Darity, Dr. Carl Hart, Basil Rahman, John Turner, Keisha Lance Bottoms for adding perspective. To everyone who I have worked with during my years in the media industry, thank you. Thanks to all artists, producers, managers, publicists, journalists, lawyers, radio DJs, promo teams, and record labels who helped to put the city of Atlanta on the map through music, entertainment, culture, and arts.

NOTES

Introduction

1. WERD Oral History and Interviews. Auburn Avenue Research Library on African-American Culture and History.
2. "Finding Value in Racism: The Spatial Choreography of Black and White in Early Twentieth Century Atlanta," PhD diss., University of Georgia, 2013.
3. "Economic Disparities in Atlantta as 'Black Mecca.'" Biz Journals. June 26, 2020.

Chapter 1

1. H.R. 5484 Anti-Drug Abuse Act
October 27, 1986 Became Law No: 99-570.
2. H.R. 3355 Violent Crime Control and Law Enforcement Act of 1994.
September 13, 1994 Became Public Law No" 103-322.
3. Interview with Dr. Carl Hart of Columbia University. October 30, 2013.
4. National Research Council. 2014. The Growth of Incarceration in the United States: Exploring Causes and Consequences. The National Academies Press.
5. "Atlanta is Making Way for New Public Housing." New York Times. June 20, 2009.
6. "Miami Boys Changing Atlanta Drug Scene. Associated Press. February 10, 1988.
7. Interview with John Turner, former Assistant District Attorney in Fulton County. October 2015.
8. "Miami Boys gain drugs foothold." Atlanta Journal-Constitution. February 3, 1988.
9. The Original Miami Boys. By James Sawyer. December 14, 2014.

Chapter 2

1. Interview with Michael Barney, founder of Magic City. December 2011.
2. Portishead's Dummy. By R.J. Wheaton. 2011.
3. Interview with Kilo Ali. August 3, 2018.
4. The Art of Organized Noize. Director Quincy Jones III. Documentary. 2016.
5. Interview with DJ Toomp. January 2015.
6. "Kilo Ali: Out of Prison, Back in the Studio." By WMGT Producer. February 14, 2011.

Chapter 3

1. Interview with Migos. March 10, 2017.
2. Interview with Big Boi. March 2016.
3. Interview with T.I. June 2018.
4. Interview with Khujo Goodie of Goodie Mob. March 2018.
5. Higher is Waiting. By Tyler Perry. 2017.
6. "Freaknik: Not just another traffic jam." Atlanta Journal-Constitution. April 16, 2010.
7. "So So Def at 20: How it all Began." Creative Loafing. February 21, 2013.

Chapter 4

1. Interview with Shawty Lo. 2011.
2. "Shawty Lo Recalls Fast-Paced Youth in His Atlanta Hood" MTV News. By Shaheem Reid. October 25, 2009.
3. "A powerful explosion blew out part of a daycare." United Press International. By Robert Rountree. October 13, 1980.
4. "Atlanta rapper Shawty Lo killed in fiery crash." Atlanta Journal-Constitution. By Lauren Foreman. September 21, 2016.

Chapter 5

1. "Rapper T.I. arrested on machine gun charges, misses BET show." CNN. By Rahul Bali. October 14, 2007.
2. "Housing project is so tough that letter carriers have police escorts." Associated Press. By Sonya Ross. December 16, 1988.
3. Interview with DJ Toomp. January 2015.
4. "Iran-Contra Hearings: 'I came to tell you the truth.'" New York Times. July 8, 1987.
5. Interview with Kawan "KP" Prather. March 2017.
6. Interview with T.I.. June 2018.
7. Interview with Killer Mike. March 2016
8. Interview with Jason Geter. January 2016
9. Interview with L.A. Reid. February 20016.

Chapter 6

1. Interview with Jeezy. October 2016.
2. Interview with DJ Drama. January 2015.
3. "Hip-Hop's shadowy empire." Creative Loafing. By Mara Shalhoup. December 2006.
4. Interview with Nick Young. February 2018.
5. Interview with DJ Toomp. January 2015.
6. "Ten Defendants Sentenced in Black Mafia Family Cocaine Distribution Case." Department of Justice. By U.S. Attorney Davide E. Nahmias. October 30, 2008.
7. "With Arrest of DJ Drama, the Law takes Aim at Mixtapes." New York Times. By Kelefa Sanneh. January 18, 2007.

Chapter 7

1. The Autobiography of Gucci Mane. By Gucci Mane. 2017

2. "Atlanta Rapper Gucci Mane faces Murder Charge." MTV News. May 23, 2005.
3. "Gucci Mane will face travel restrictions on release from prison." Atlanta Journal-Constitution. August 20, 2014.
4. Interview with Young Scooter. March 2013.
5. Interview with Gucci Mane. March 2013.
6. Interview with Young Thug. June 2015.
7. Interview with Killer Mike. May 2018.
8. Interview with Zaytoven. June 2018.

Chapter 8

1. Coach K's Masterclass, Morehouse College. April 2018.
2. Interview with Zaytoven. June 2018.
3. Interview with Miss Rici. March 2018.
4. "'Atlanta' wins Golden Globe for Best TV Series Comedy." Variety. Geoff Berkshire. January 8, 2017.
5. Interview with Donald Glover. February 2018.
6. Interview with Migos. April 2017.

Chapter 9

1. "Police Kill Woman, 92, in Shootout at her Home." New York Times. By Brenda Goodman. November 23, 2006.
2. Interview with Curtis Snow. May 2011.
3. Interview with Killer Mike. March 2016.

Chapter 10

1. Interview with Kareem, resident of the Bluff. July 2017.
2. Interview with Gary, resident of the Bluff. July 2017.
3. Interview with Mona Bennett, co-founder of the AHRC. July 2017.
4. President Obama's speaks at AmericasMart in Atlanta, Georgia. March 2016

5. HIV Surveillance Report, 2016; vol. 28. Centers for Disease Control and Prevention. Published November 2017.
6. Interview with Basil Abdur-Rahman. February 2010.
7. Interview with Shanti Das. December 2017.

Chapter 11

1. "Man found not guilty of murder in Slim Dunkin's death." Atlanta Journal-Constitution. By Marcus K. Garner. February 25, 2013.

2. "Rapper Doe B Shot and Killed in Alabama." Billboard. December 2013.
3. "Doe B remembered at his funeral in Alabama." Rolling Out magazine. By A.R. Shaw. December 2013.
4. "Final Centennial Hill shooting defendant sentenced to 15 years." Montgomery Advertiser. By Kirsten Fiscus. September 13, 2018.
5. "Rapper Bankroll Fresh Killed in shooting at Atlanta studio." Atlanta Journal-Constitution. By Tyler Estep. March 2016.
6. "Bankroll Fresh remembered at funeral in Atlanta." Rolling Out magazine. By A.R. Shaw. March 2016.
7. "Nipsey Hussle takes final ride as thousands line streets of Los Angeles." Rolling Out magazine. By A.R. Shaw. April. 2019.

Chapter 12

1. Interview with Future. June 2012.
2. "Pratt-Pullman Yard, one of Atlanta's largest and most historic sites, now belongs to Hollywood." Atlanta Magazine. By Josh Green. November 2017.
3. "As Atlanta Changes, Mayoral Candidates take on Gentrification." Wall Street Journal. By Cameron McWhirter. November 2017.

4. "Atlanta's 'Berlin Wall.'" Atlanta Magazine. By Paul Carter. December 2011.
5. "Beltline creator Gravel resigns from Partnership." Atlanta Journal-Constitution. September 2016.
6. "Jamestown CEO: Gentrification Complicated." Atlanta Jewish Times. By David R. Cho. June 2017.
7. "Right-wing gentrification gangs." Atlanta Antifascists. August 2017.
8. Interview with T.I. November 2017.

Chapter 13

1. Interview with 2 Chainz. November 2019 .
2. Interview with Antwanette McLaughlin, curator of Trap Music Museum. September 2018.
3. Interview with Maya Bailey, artist and curator of Trap Music Museum. September 2018.

Chapter 14

1. Interview with DJ White Shadow. April 2015.
2. "Flosstradamus shares their thoughts Trap music." High Snobiety. August 2016.
3. Interview with DJ Gün. April 2015.
4. Interview with DJ Toomp. January 2015.
5. Interview with Jeezy. October 2016.
6. Interview with Mthembeni "Emtee" Ndevuo.

Chapter 15

1. Interview with Bobby Rush. August 2016.
2. Interview with Sammy Blues. September 2016.
3. Interview with Dr. William Darity, Jr. May 2017.
4. Interview with Killer Mike. March 2016.
5. Interview with Jeezy. October 2016.
6. Interview with Keisha Lance Bottoms. December 2017.

ABOUT THE AUTHOR

A.R. Shaw is an author, journalist, and filmmaker, who documents culture, politics, and entertainment. He has over a decade of experience in the field of media and has published essays and articles on the Obama White House, the Summer Olympics in London, and Atlanta's ever-growing music scene. Shaw is the creator of the podcast "Trap History" and is currently working on a new book and film.

Follow A.R. Shaw:
Instagram: @arshaw23
Instagram: @TrapHistory
Twitter: @arshaw
www.traphistory.com

www.ingramcontent.com/pod-product-compliance
Lightning Source LLC
LaVergne TN
LVHW041541070426
835507LV00011B/856